Great Advice!

Your 7 KEYS To A Better Life!

Michael B. Davie

Manor House Publishing

Great Advice! / Michael B. Davie

Library and Archives Canada
Cataloguing in Publication

Davie, Michael B., 1954-
Great Advice! : *Your 7 KEYS To A Better Life*!
/ Michael B. Davie

ISBN 978-1-988058-32-0 (softcover)

ISBN 978-1-988058-33-7 (hardcover)

1. Self-actualization (Psychology) / self-help / home ownership / Starting a Business / I. Title.

BF637.S4C395 2018   158.1   C2018-906209-6

First Main Edition

Copyright: 2018
Cover main art photo: Shutterstock

Published by Manor House Publishing Inc.
4522 Cottingham Crescent, Ancaster, Ontario, Canada, L9G 3V6
905-648-2193
www.manor-house-publishing.com

All rights reserved.

Great Advice! / Michael B. Davie

For those who are starting out in life, starting a family, a career, home ownership or starting a business – and for those who are downsizing and starting retirement – for anyone and everyone experiencing a new phase of life and looking for great advice – this book is for all of you.

Great Advice! / Michael B. Davie

Great Advice! / Michael B. Davie

Acknowledgements:

To my wife Philippa, to the Canadian, US and UK distributors for Manor House and to the experts who provided key advice on a range of life-changing topics – Samantha Cervino, Victoria Lorient-Faibish, Rebecca Rosenblat, Blythe Ward, Paula Hope, Susan Crossman and others, my thanks to you all.

TABLE OF CONTENTS

Foreword   9

Chapter-Key 1: Own Your Home: 17
This is absolutely key at any stage of life – but the sooner the better. Owning your home means you're investing in yourself instead of paying rent to a landlord. It means you're building equity via an investment that grows in value – while at the same time you have the added benefit of living in that investment. Later on, you can sell this investment and invest in another home or finance something else of value, such as your retirement. Home ownership helps people of ordinary means, even those of limited means, achieve wealth, prosperity, income security.

Chapter-Key 2: Get a Good Job: 45
Now it's time to start a Full-time job with enough income to support an independent lifestyle – with careful budgeting It may also be time to start a career – here's advice on how to go about choosing/building the career that's right for you

Chapter-Key 3: Mine Your Own Business: 57
Yes, that's *mine* your own business as a small business can be a virtual gold mine of extra wealth, extracting a secondary or even primary source of income while providing a strong source of satisfaction and enjoyment – truly a rewarding experience, but you need to do it right. More and more in these uncertain times, job security is an outdated notion. Having a secondary source of income via a business is a wise move – and if it grows enough to fully support you, why not seize the option of living your dream and being your own boss?

Chapter-Key 4: Build Your Brand with Marketing   79
Even before you start a business, you should have a sense of your market and demand for the goods and/or services you'll offer. Once you have the business up and running for a few months, a marketing plan is a vital means to exploit your market, bring in revenue and make your business grow.

Chapter-Key 5: Live Healthy: 95

Your health is of paramount importance – yet it's often overshadowed by financial or social concerns. But little else matters if you don't have your health. Throughout your life you need to have in place the healthy practices and routines to keep your physically fit and feeling your best. This includes getting enough sleep and exercise to keep you alert and strong. It also includes well balanced diet and regular medical care. Here's Great Advice to keep you strong and healthy throughout your life and ready to take on each day with vigour and enthusiasm.

Chapter-Key 6: Further Your Education: 109

Education has long been an established key to personal success, to achieving a good-paying job and-or career. It's important to decide what you want to do in life and select courses that will give you the knowledge and credentials to help you pursue your dream. Beyond the positive contribution of education on your job, career and income stream, furthering your education provides the added benefits of helping you grow as a person, develop analytical skills, learn to view things from different perspectives and more. Your education should be a matter of life-long learning as you expand your understanding of your life and the world around you.

Chapter-Key 7: Nurture Your Relationships: 118

Building happy, loving relationships is what life is all about. Financial success means little if our relationship with our self, friends and family is rooted in unhappiness. After all, what is the point of achieving career success and accumulating wealth if our core being is ill at ease, if our home is a place of tension and animosity. We need to find joy and fulfillment within ourselves and through our relationships with others. It's vitally important that our relationships be based on good communication coupled with realistic expectations and a willingness to work things out, so that we share a calm, successful state of serenity.

About the Author 143

About the Publisher 144

Great Advice! / Michael B. Davie

Foreword

The most important part of any journey is that first step.

Risk of failure is greatest when you're starting something new. It's your first time and you don't have a road map – until now: ***Great Advice! – Your 7 Keys to a Better life!*** is your breakthrough whole-life handbook.

Some books offer financial advice; others offer relationship advice. But ***Great Advice!*** has it all. It's the one book you need to make all the right financial and relationship moves.

Although this book definitely helps young people, rest assured that you don't have to be a young person starting out to benefit from this book – the advice in these pages applies to people in any stage of life – and any nationality.

Perhaps you're middle-aged or older and feel you've missed the boat to change your life for the better – the good news is this: You have *not* missed the boat: It's not too late to make needed changes to improve your life now and in future years.

If you're part of an older generation – even approaching retirement – your timeframe for making changes may be a little shorter, but it's truly amazing and encouraging what success keys you can still achieve in the short-term and somewhat longer-term, including the success keys of home-ownership, improved education, starting a small business and marketing plan, better health, and improving relationships with loved ones.

Young or old, this book is here to help you get the most out of life and live a comfortable, satisfying and rewarding life.

Whether you or a loved one is starting out in life or whether you're in a later stage of life; whether you or a loved one is starting a career, starting home ownership, starting a family, or starting retirement, key advice you need is right here in one remarkable book, sharing tips and valuable insights from leading experts from regional, national and international organizations, companies and agencies.

Great Advice! is your best source of expert advice from those who know. It's your guidebook to survive and thrive when starting any new passage in life and it steers you clear of making costly mistakes.

For any stage of your life, here's the help you need to start smart – and lay a firm foundation for a lifetime of success, utilizing the seven keys to a comfortable, prosperous life:

The following 7 Keys are in no particular order as all of them should be worked on simultaneously. Having said that, I've listed the Home Ownership key first as this key truly makes a difference for anyone of ordinary means for gaining wealth and prosperity. Renters can still prosper utilizing the other keys but the home-ownership key is the biggest wealth-generator. Here now are the 7 Keys:

KEY 1: Own Your Home: This is absolutely key at any stage of life – but the sooner the better. Owning your home means you're investing in yourself instead of paying rent to a landlord. It means you're building equity via an investment that grows in value – while at the same time you have the added benefit of living in that investment. Later on, you can sell this investment and invest in another home or finance something else of value, such as your retirement. Home ownership helps people of ordinary means, even those of very limited means, achieve wealth, prosperity and income security.

KEY 2: Get A Good Job: This is also vitally important of course. Most people of ordinary means don't have an estate or inheritance and do need a job to survive. But your job should do more than just pay the bills. You want to achieve more than simply living paycheque-to-paycheque. If the pay level is low, you nonetheless want to manage your income to pay the bills AND allow you to accumulate funds for a down payment on a home and perhaps start-up funds for a small business – while still leaving some cash for an occasional night out. You also want to have a job or career doing work you enjoy doing, something you find satisfying and rewarding. Most people typically spend at least half their awake life at work – make sure you enjoy it.

KEY 3: Mine Your Own Business: Yes, that's *mine* your own business as a small business can be a virtual gold mine of extra wealth, extracting a secondary or even primary source of income while providing a strong source of satisfaction and enjoyment – truly a rewarding experience, but you need to do it right. More and more in these uncertain times, job security is an outdated notion. Having a secondary source of income via a business is a wise move – and if it grows enough to fully support you, why not seize the option of living your dream and being your own boss?

KEY 4: Build Your Brand with Marketing: Even before you start a business, you should have a sense of your market and demand for the goods and/or services you'll offer. Once you have the business up and running for a few months, a marketing plan is a vital means to exploit your market, bring in revenue and make your business grow. Here's what you need to know to set up a marketing plan tailor-made for your business now and in the future.

KEY 5: Live Healthy: Your health is of paramount importance – yet it's often overshadowed by financial or social concerns. But little else matters if you don't have your health. Throughout your life you need to have in place the healthy practices and routines to keep your physically fit and feeling your best. This includes getting enough sleep and exercise to keep you alert and strong. It also includes well balanced diet and regular medical care. Here's Great Advice to keep you strong and healthy throughout your life and ready to take on each day with vigour and enthusiasm.

KEY 6: Further Your Education: Education has long been an established key to personal success, to achieving a good-paying job and-or career. It's important to decide what you want to do in life and select courses that will give you the knowledge and credentials to help you pursue your dream. Beyond the positive contribution of education on your job, career and income stream, furthering your education provides the added benefits of helping you grow as a person, develop analytical skills, learn to view things from different perspectives and more. Your education should be a matter of life-long learning as you expand your understanding of your life and the world around you.

KEY 7: Nurture Your Relationships:
Building happy, loving relationships is what life is all about. Financial success means little if our relationship with our self and others is rooted in unhappiness. After all, what is the point of achieving career success and accumulating wealth if our core being is ill at ease, if our home is a place of tension and animosity. We need to find joy and fulfillment within ourselves and through our relationships with others. It's vitally important that our relationships be based on good communication coupled with realistic expectations and a willingness to work things out, so that we share a calm, successful state of serenity.

If you or a loved one is just starting out:

So, you've left your parents' home – or perhaps one of your children has just left your home: One thing for certain: Anyone leaving their parents' home for the first time is usually in for a rude awakening.

The outside world is a strange and challenging place that lacks supportive parents, living accommodations at little or no cost, laundry services, home-cooked meals and access to the family car.

Many young people venturing out on their own make the same common mistakes: They get a "free" cell phone with a usage plan and cancellation fees they can't afford; a new vehicle with payments they can't afford; an apartment they can't afford and an unrealistic lifestyle they also can't afford. That's all partly because there isn't a manual they can turn to for the right advice – until now.

If you're not attending college or university, consider on-the-job training for a career in an industry that interests you. (automotive sales, mechanics; electrician; plumber; tool-and-die; etc.) Once you attain full status, these can be high paying jobs that can deliver a fulfilling lifestyle.

Consider an affordable used car, rather than a new one that'll lock you into payments for several years or more.

Many of the above points will be discussed in more detail in the chapters ahead – the key theme here is this: Rather than embark on a costly unaffordable lifestyle, you need to cut costs wherever possible so you not only cover all costs but are also left with a disposable income you can then invest in home ownership, a business and more to build your wealth - and improve your relationships and your life.

If you or a loved one is middle-aged or older:

So, you're middle-aged or older - or you know someone who is – and you're thinking this book can't help someone this late in life – well, please think again. The timeframe may be shorter due to age, but you can still improve your life considerably utilizing the advice in this book.

For example, buying a home when you're in your thirties, forties or even fifties can still give you a decade or more of home ownership, during which time you're paying down the mortgage, increasing your equity – and your equity will also grow due to normal annual appreciation increases in the market value of your home.

And if any of your relationships are in trouble or lacking in any way, this book will help you find the path to happiness at any stage in your life.

Sharing Advice: A Business Opportunity for Experts:

The advice in this book is meant to be shared to help as many as possible – and it's available via sellers globally with bestseller status expected soon after its release.

Widespread sharing between friends and family is also a given as someone needing home-buying advice may then lend their copy to someone else needing similar advice or relationship help or small business advice etc.

Great Advice! provides people of various backgrounds and ages with expert advice to help those of even ordinary means achieve wealth, security and relationship happiness.

As such, it also makes an excellent helpful goodwill gift to clients and prospective clients of realtors-real estate agents, mortgage brokers, educators, relationship counselors, business consultants, health care professionals and others committed to helping people lead better lives. As each of these experts distributes books they're promoting not only themselves, but the other featured experts as well.

Gifting copies not only helps the recipient but also the giver, who gains more lasting promotional benefit and goodwill credibility than advertising could ever provide.

Experts desiring a complementary full-page Source write-up in this book to reach out to and help their local customers should contact author Michael B. Davie at mbdavie@manorhouse.biz to discuss and obtain a simple application form attesting they're of good character with no claims-judgments against them and are primarily interested in advising-helping others succeed. The write-up is free with the purchase of copies to distribute to others.

Wherever you live in the world - this book is for You!

Whether you're Canadian, American, British, Australian, Asian, European, or another nationality, it's a certainty you'll benefit substantially from the advice in this book.

Certainly the advice on relationships is both universal and timeless regardless of where you live in the world.

While the business and real estate advice is fairly universal, you'll need to research your regional, provincial or state markets and available programs for your specific locale.

As you embark on the next part of your journey, I thank you for taking *Great Advice!* along with you – and I wish you much success in all aspects of your life.
- **Michael B. Davie**

Great Advice! / Michael B. Davie

Great Advice! / Michael B. Davie

Chapter-Key 1
Own Your Home

This is absolutely key at any stage of life – but the sooner the better. Owning your home means you're investing in yourself instead of paying rent to a landlord. It means you're building equity via an investment that grows in value – while at the same time you have the added benefit of living in that investment. Later on, you can sell this investment and invest in another home or finance something else of value, such as your retirement. Home ownership helps people of ordinary means, even those of limited means, achieve wealth, prosperity, income security.

Here's the advice you need on choosing the best affordable housing type, location, budgeting, big down-payment, moving, using a mortgage broker and real estate agent, terms, things to watch out for, interest rates, hidden costs, etc. Plus: advice on starting downsizing later in life.

Home ownership is the biggest single financial investment most people will ever make in their lifetime. It's also your key to wealth and a comfortable life, now and in retirement.

The advantages of ownership over renting are many: An owner has control and possession of a valuable asset while a renter has no control or possession of any asset and can face rent hikes and even eviction should the owner decide to sell even if rent payments have been kept up.

A homeowner has the added benefit of enjoyment of living in their investment. Instead of paying a landlord, the owner makes mortgage payments that steadily increase their ownership stake until they own 100% of the asset. They then have the option of downsizing to a less-expensive dwelling they can buy outright, investing the difference in a retirement fund paying income while living mortgage-free.

As with any major decision, making the right moves at the outset – starting smart – is especially important when it comes to deciding on an investment that literally determines where you live.

It's often said buying a home is the single expenditure and the single biggest investment most people will ever make. It's also one of most important decisions you'll ever make.

Home ownership is truly an investment in yourself, diverting rent money that would go to a landlord to instead add directly to your own personal wealth with your own nest egg that grows in value year after year.

It's also an unusual investment as you get to derive the added benefits of living in your home and enjoying all it has to offer while you chip away at the mortgage – perhaps paying it off completely – while building wealth.

On retiring, you have the added option of selling your home, downsizing to a smaller abode worth less, and investing the difference to finance your retirement.

So, with all of this in mind, it's vitally important that you make the right moves to achieve home ownership.

This chapter will provide great advice on the key aspects of home-buying and selling, home-ownership and downsizing.

Real estate markets vary from city to city, town to town, country to country, with some communities more in demand than others, driving prices upward.

But real estate experts agree there are some basic universal common guidelines you'll want to follow:

Cost-Cutting Tips to Achieve Home Ownership:

You need to pay off your debts and live within your means, thereby increasing the income you have to finance home ownership. This may seem like a daunting if not impossible task, but here are some steps you can take to accumulate a good down payment over the next 3-5 years even if you're now barely getting by, living paycheque to paycheque:

1. Pay off debt: Credit card debt must go and avoid taking on any further high interest debt – it's eating into your income and hurting your credit rating. You can do this! It's largely a matter of cutting non-essential costs such as dining out, expensive vacations (opt for local day trips), and shopping trips that aren't necessary and tend to jack up your credit card costs. If you're carrying a large debt-load, you may not even qualify for a mortgage.

2. Cut Unnecessary costs: For example, if you can get by without a car then sell your vehicle and use public transit (or walk to work if it's within hiking distance). You can put the revenue from the sale of your vehicle towards a down payment on a home while also saving a fortune in vehicle payments, insurance, repairs, license, plates and maintenance. If you must have a car, at least make it as economical as possible – a dependable older vehicle for example that you can buy outright as opposed to a costly new car with payments that drain your disposable income. And if you have two cars, you can at least cut back to one.

3. Reduce Rent Costs: If you're currently renting an apartment, consider taking in a roommate who will pay at least half the costs of rent, utilities etc., thereby allowing you to set aside money for a home purchase (if you and your partner are buying a home together, share an apartment to cut costs) Moving from a 2-bedroom to a 1 bedroom or even a bachelor apartment can also cut costs when a roommate isn't an option. Or simply moving to a less costly apartment in a still decent neighbourhood can make a difference. And, likely one of the most effective ways to live inexpensively: Temporarily move back home with your parents. Don't cringe – you may not have got on that well in the past, but you've grown up since then. Talk to your folks and you may be surprised at how receptive they'll be to having you back, but this time as a responsible adult who can help out with chores and kick in a bit for room and board while still saving BIG for home ownership.

4. Quit Smoking: Smokers who quit can also save thousands of dollars a year – and cutting back on alcohol consumption is also a cost-saver.

5. Take the Free Way: Enjoy Free shows / entertainment over costly paid shows – and go for other 'free' options such as borrowing library books instead of buying books – and you can likely think of other frugal ways you can cut costs and save money, while still enjoying yourself.

The five preceding listed approaches to cost-cutting will help you to not only raise funds for a down-payment but will also help you carry your housing costs after purchase.

Beyond cost-cutting of course, you can also raise additional funds via supplementary or freelance employment at least for a while, to generate additional funds on the supply side. This can also include extra money from a raise or bonus via your employer or business venture.

Once you've lowered your living costs, put your surplus money towards your down payment to make it as big as possible and your mortgage as small as possible – saving you thousands of dollars over the life of your mortgage.

Get Pre-approved for A Mortgage:

Once you've got your finances in order to the best of your ability and saved some money for a down payment, your next step is to get pre-approved for a mortgage based on your down payment, credit rating-score and income.

Pre-approval is crucial – it sets the maximum amount of mortgage money you can borrow, so you're not wasting time looking at houses you can't buy. In fact, most real estate agents won't work with anyone not pre-approved..

Let's say you've managed to save $50,000 in five years – a 20 per cent down payment on a $250,000 home (it may just be a fixer-upper or condo depending on your local market).

For Canadians, a 20 per cent down payment was once fairly common but with today's higher house prices it's now somewhat rare. But if you have less than 20 per cent down you'll have to pay mandatory mortgage default Insurance from CMHC (Canada Mortgage and Housing Corporation).

CMHC's mortgage default insurance allows you to buy a home and take on a mortgage if your down payment is less than 20 per cent –even as low as the 5 per cent minimum –

but a CMHC-insured mortgage is a costly option that doesn't protect you. It protects the lender if you default.

Using our $250,000 purchase price example, a 5 per cent – or $12,500 – down payment means you'll pay $7,481 in CMHC insurance that's added onto your mortgage and paid off over the life of your mortgage. So, although you put $12,500 down, reducing your mortgage to $237,500 the additional $7,481 insurance jacked the total back up to $244,981. But if you had instead put $50,000 down, you'd pay no insurance and your mortgage is just $200,000.

The importance of a good down payment cannot be over emphasized – you avoid having to pay default insurance, your down payment goes purely against the principle to significantly lower the total size of your mortgage and you can pay off your smaller mortgage sooner with payments that may more affordable while still cutting nicely into the principle amount owed. Some jurisdictions also provide a tax credit to first-time buyers (in Ontario it's up to $750).

Using our Cost-Cutting Tips to Achieve Home Ownership, you may be able to set aside $800 a month – which over the course of 5 years adds up to a $50,000 down payment that in turn makes your payments more affordable. If you can get your mortgage payments to where they're comparable to rent while you're cutting into principle – you're winning.

If you haven't managed to save the down payment you need, there may be the option of taking out a bank loan. Some jurisdictions also have programs to assist first-time homebuyers. Canada's Home Buyers' Plan lets first-timers borrow up to $25,000 from their Registered Retirement Savings Plans to finance a down payment, provided they repay the loan within 15 years. However, be aware these options mean taking on additional payments. You'll also have to pay closing costs (these can include home inspection fees, legal fees, land transfer tax, etc.) and there are the other costs of home ownership, such as property taxes, hydro, sewer-water, maintenance and insurance. So, plan and prepare for the full array of costs – but know that it adds to your financial burden to take on loan payments in addition to mortgage payments and all your other costs.

Getting pre-approved for a mortgage means you're now operating from a position of strength and confidence. You know exactly how much you can borrow and you can use that information to guide you in your quest for a home.

Use A Mortgage Broker:

You can go to your bank to get pre-approved and take out a mortgage with them – but in most cases you're far better off getting your pre-approval and mortgage through a reputable mortgage broker, who will shop the mortgage market for you and get you a better deal that you can get on your own – even from your own bank.

"Whether the client is financially successful or is currently facing financial issues, we can save them some money by shopping the mortgage market to find a deal that best meets their needs," mortgage broker Ken Lindsay, president of Mortgage Financial Corporation, explains in an interview at company headquarters on Ray Street South, Hamilton.

"There aren't too many people who can go to a bank – even their own bank – and get a better deal than we can," Mr. Lindsay asserts. "That's because we're able to exercise a fair amount of buying power, some real financial clout, given the amount of business we bring to the banks."

"And for those customers who have been turned down by a bank, we're often able to get them a mortgage – sometimes from the same bank that turned them down – by negotiating a deal that works for everyone," adds Mr. Lindsay.

Financial lenders, including banks and trust companies, pay the firm a finder's fee/commission for bringing them ready-to-go mortgage deals for financially secure borrowers.

The arrangement also works well for banks, which rely on the broker to bring them mortgage business. The bank gets to sit back while the broker does the bulk of the work. And the bank will withhold any commission until the successful completion of a mortgage deal.
"It's basically a risk-free undertaking for the banks – it's really good for all of the financial institutions," Mr. Lindsay notes, "and the banks remain suppliers of the mortgage funds in most cases."

"Usually we can negotiate a deal at virtually no cost to the mortgage-borrower – they literally have nothing to lose and everything to gain with lower rates and better terms," Mr. Lindsay says, noting these clients account for about 75 per cent of his business, "and we can sometimes even beat the rates the banks offer their own staff."

And there's hope for would-be homeowners with credit difficulties who have been turned down by the banks: Mortgage Financial charges a fee to less-secure clients to arrange a mortgage, normally at somewhat higher interest rates to reflect the added degree of risk involved.

"Even for clients who aren't financially secure, we can often put together a deal that's not a whole lot more expensive than what someone in a more financially advantageous position would be taking on," he adds. "It comes down to the volume of business we do – it's buying power."

Even a modest difference in interest rates can prove substantial. For example, before factoring in property taxes, a small $100,000 mortgage, amortized over 20 years (the full lifespan of the mortgage) at a 3 per cent interest rate would cost the borrower $554 in monthly principal-and-interest payments. But the same mortgage with a 4 per cent interest rate would push the monthly payment to more than $600. And at 5 per cent, the monthly payment needed increases to $660. A further increase of less than one per cent – to 5.75 per cent – inflates the monthly payments to $700 (numbers are much higher with a $200,000 mortgage) Ideally your mortgage payments will be comparable to what you were paying in rent. But even if they're more, the benefits of home ownership are worth the added cost.

Here, Mortgage Financial broker-agents routinely save their clients many thousands of dollars in mortgage payments annually by arranging lower-rate mortgages. "We can benefit the customer, whether they're well-off or have financial concerns by shopping the market to get them the best mortgage terms and rates," Mr. Lindsay asserts.

"If they're well-off, we can get them better rates and terms than they'll likely be able to get on their own," adds Mr. Lindsay, whose company puts together thousands mortgages a year – worth over $100-million – and has 30 per cent annual growth.

"If the client is struggling or working through financial issues, we can, in most cases, get them a pretty good mortgage when they otherwise might not be able to get any mortgage at all," he adds. "The secret of our success is getting into the minds of the clients and getting the detailed information we need to help them. It's our job to know what people need – not the customer's job to find out – we're valued for our opinion and expertise; it's our job."

Mr. Lindsay says bank turn-downs account for 10 to 15 per cent of business and turning these deals around often involves creatively thinking outside the box to structure deals with co-signers or other arrangements that reduce risk and make banks more likely to lend. He notes his ability to draw on a number of lenders means he can offer just about any mortgage package combination imaginable. "If you, as an individual, are still limiting yourself to one lending institution, you pretty much have to take what you can get and that's not always the best deal that's out there."

To relate my personal story as author of this book: My wife and I used Ken's services years ago and were surprised he could get better terms than we could from our own bank! We chose an MCAP mortgage (Bank of Montreal) with weekly payments (monthly payment is divided in four and since many months have five weeks, you pay down more principle) along with the flexibility to make extra payments against principal at any time – within a few years we'd paid off our mortgage and to this day we remain mortgage-free!

More Canadians are coming to see the inherent value of arranging mortgages through a broker. However, in Canada the percentage of people taking this route is just 35 per cent – well behind the U.S. rate of 85 per cent – but the rate is growing more people discover the many benefits of using a mortgage broker.

Clients also benefit from Mr. Lindsay's access to a large pool of lenders, the negotiating clout his volume of business gives him with the banks, his industry savvy and his ability to negotiate a win-win deal for client and lender.

"We can custom tailor a mortgage to the customer's needs right off the bat because we have so many lenders and mortgage products to choose from," he notes. "It's a great feeling when we're able to get someone a terrific interest rate and terms – and it's a great feeling when someone who figured they'd never be able to buy a home gets a mortgage through us and achieves the dream of home ownership."

To tailor a mortgage to the client's needs, Mr. Lindsay or one of his broker-agents will sit down with the customer and determine what their income levels are, how much mortgage they can afford to carry, what payment schedules are best-suited for them, how determined they are to pay off the mortgage and other options are worth considering.

For example, mortgage options can include the length of amortization – whether the total mortgage life span runs 10, 15, 20 or 25 years. A shorter amortization means the mortgage is paid off entirely much more quickly, but the weekly or monthly payments are much higher than they would be with a longer amortization period.

However, regardless of the amortization, weekly payments (or payments every two weeks) are often recommended as they effectively translate into an extra monthly payment each year, which in turn means the mortgage is being reduced a little more quickly and conveniently.

Mortgage options can include a number of variations in the length of the term – whether one wants to go six months, one year, two years, three years or five years before renewing the mortgage.

The borrower may also want to knock down the size of the mortgage by having extra payment privileges that allow for larger payments or a lump sum payment or both during the mortgage term.

There are still also mortgage variations, including fixed rates that lock you in at a set interest rate for the mortgage term, and variable rates, which are tied to market interest rates and follow those rates up or down.

Variable rates are often considered attractive to borrowers if they anticipate rates remaining low or falling. But if rates rise, the borrower pays the higher rate.

Fixed rates are sometimes a little more costly, but they provide the stability of certainty over the level of interest rate the borrower will pay.

Use A Realtor:

So, you're now pre-approved for a mortgage, you know how much you can spend on a home purchase, and you're also comfortable with the other costs of home-ownership. Now you can begin to search for a home – but whether you're buying your first home or selling a home and buying another, you're always well advised to use a realtor.

After all, why would you want to spend an enormous amount of your time driving around, searching for, and arranging to see homes to buy (and the seller will want to be home for any tour by a non-agent)? You don't need that kind of headache – why not let a professional help you with this and find an affordable home that's right for you?

If you're selling in addition to buying, any amount you might save in agent commission fees could be more than erased by a shortfall in revenue by not getting the best price for your house – and you'll also be paying for your own advertising-promotion-signage.

Great Advice! / Michael B. Davie

If you're not selling but only buying, the agent commission is not an issue as the seller alone pays it. But in either case, you're best to let a real estate professional shepherd you through this journey: It only makes sense to use a realtor who can provide the time, knowledge, expertise, advice and market access via MLS (Multiple Listing Service) you need to navigate the real estate market.

Most realtors also have a network of other folks you'll need to make a home purchase happen, such as lawyers, home inspectors, insurers, mortgage brokers etc. – sometimes offering their services at lower rates due to the volume of business they do with the realtor. Making this move takes a heavy burden of worry off your mind.

When choosing an agent, ask for referrals and-or consider an agent that friends or family members have used in the past and recommend.

You also need to make sure you're going with a licensed real estate professional, who has completed the requisite intensive course of study and is a member of a local real estate association, such as the Realtors Association of Hamilton-Burlington, with over 3,000 members who are held to a high standard as real estate professionals who subscribe to a strict code of professional ethics.

A good realtor will also make your home hunt an enjoyable fun experience. My wife and I really looked forward to our agent picking us up and taking us out to explore the latest array of homes the agent had arranged for us to view.

So what should you look for in a home? The three most important things, according to the old real estate cliché are: Location, location, location – and there's no question a good location is vitally important. You want to live in safe neighborhood, perhaps close to where you work, likely on a quiet, rather than busy, street. You may also want to be close to schools, close to parks and shopping, a short drive or even walking distance to friends and family – you need to determine what's most important to you in a home's location.

As we've discussed, affordability is also essential – and on this front you may want to consider compromising on the type of home you're looking for: A fully detached home in a great neighborhood may check most of your boxes – but if it's not affordable, you may find yourself house-poor, with nearly all of your available income going to your home, leaving little left for a night out.

Choosing a semi-detached home or even a townhouse can give you a lot more home for a lot less money, allowing you to enjoy life with disposable income for entertainment – while you also enjoy your home, regardless of whether it's fully detached or not (but be aware that your lower-priced semi-detached house, townhouse or condo apartment may appreciate at a slower rate than a detached home).

Beyond your realtor, a key member of your support team you'll need to hire is a lawyer to scrutinize the financial transaction, review the purchase document, ensure property taxes are paid up to date, ensure there are no claims or liens against the property and verify the deed to the property is valid and that you have free and clear title to the property.

Hiring a home inspector can also be a good move as the inspector will alert you to any issues. Should issues be found, you've been warned in advance of buying the home. You can then decide whether you still want to buy and whether you can afford the cost to remedy the issue or issues uncovered. You can also use this information to bargain for a lower purchase price. Better to spend a few hundred dollars for a thorough inspection by a licensed professional than to forego this cost and perhaps discover very costly problems later on.

Your real estate agent may be able to recommend a good home inspector, who will then look at a range of things, including state of the roof, water leaks and damage to ceilings and walls, and more.

With your team in place, you're ready to go house-hunting. I recommend always searching for a home with the significant other you'll be sharing it with. That sounds obvious but there are cases where one party wanted to surprise the other with a new home, only to find their partner complained the kitchen and/or bathrooms were too small or had issues with the home's layout or location.

Another approach I highly recommend is to imagine yourself living in each home you look at. This again may sound obvious, but it can be easy to become seduced by the look in a nicely staged living room, that's perhaps sparsely furnished with a few small pieces of furniture. You need to ask yourself if your own coach will fit nicely in this space.

You also need to imagine your coffee table in this living room and if there's comfortable space to walk around it. Where will your TV go? Also, is this a room that people need to walk through to get to other rooms? If so, how long will it be before people constantly walking in front of your favourite TV show drives you crazy. Look closely at the layout of each home and see if renovations are needed, and if so, what the likely time and costs are to transform spaces.

How about the kitchen? Is there ample space here? Can you open the fridge door, dishwasher door and stove without one or more of them hitting the other? Can two or more people be in this space without bumping in to each other?

Is the main bathroom and/or ensuite big enough for two? Does it have the features you're looking for – perhaps a bathtub as well as a stand-up shower, spacious double-sink vanity, taps that don't drip and shut water off easily?

You should be prepared to compromise on small things – such as room colours you detest – you can always paint them later – and if the home is functional, you can also hold off on renovating the kitchen or bathroom until later on when you may be in a better position financially.

Of course you'll also want to ensure the home you buy meets your needs now and in the future, a home you can grow into – so if you have children or are planning a family, you'll want a home with at least three bedrooms.
Although there are usually lots of three bedroom homes in the market, four-bedroom home can be harder to find, but in any case, allow a few months for your home-search.

A good real estate agent will know the market well and be able to advise you on making an offer.

If you're in something of a Buyer's Market, there are generally more homes for sale than there are buyers, so with supply outstripping demand, you may advised to make an offer below asking price and save.

It's the reverse situation in a Seller's Market where the supply of homes is tight and in some cases there may even be bidding wars. In those markets, you may want to offer full list price to help secure the deal – but get your agent's views on this in any case.

A key goal after acquiring home-ownership should be a mortgage-free and debt-free life that frees up more money for travel and to simply enjoy all that life has to offer.

You'll need to work out your own comfort level in paying down your mortgage at a rate that allows you to make progress in this regard without resorting to a frugal existence. It's a balancing act that should allow both debt reduction, payment of bills and enjoyment of vacations and entertainment.

At some point, you'll also want to retire – and your home can then become a key part of your retirement income. You can sell it, downsize to a less expensive home and invest the difference to further finance your retirement with added income, trips, entertainment, and more – the good life!

You can also take out at your bank a HELOC (Home Equity Line of Credit) secured by your home, allowing you to borrow up to half your home's value at very low interest rates – great for covering unexpected costs (there are also reverse mortgages that don't require any payments while you reside at your home but do charge higher interest rates and can leave little for you or your estate when you sell or pass away as years of deferred payments and interest charges are due – I don't recommend reverse mortgages).

Yes, buying a home is likely the biggest purchase and biggest investment you'll ever make, a key component of your wealth gathered over your lifetime, a nest egg, and an important source of future retirement income

Simply put, owning a home is crucial to your financial success and your financial freedom from landlords. It helps you build wealth while you get the added benefits of residing within your investment.

This chapter has provided you with some key tips and a good understanding of what's involved in making one of the most important decisions of your life. It's also given you the information you need to put an action plan in place to achieve your home-ownership dream.

With your action plan in place, your next move should be contacting a mortgage broker and a reputable realtor of your choice who can guide you through your next steps.

For your convenience and consideration, we've also listed some recommended local professionals in our Sources for Great Advice section at the close of this chapter. They're just a phone call away and will happily provide you with some free expert advice as you embark on your house hunt.

Tips from CREA:

The Canadian Real Estate Association (CREA) is one of Canada's largest single-industry trade associations, representing more than 96,000 real estate Brokers/agents and salespeople working through more than 100 real estate Boards and Associations who adhere to the Realtor Code's Set standards of conduct for all real estate practitioners.

CREA owns the MLS (Multiple Listing Service) and realtor trademarks, which signify a high standard of service and also identify the members of CREA.

Great Advice! / Michael B. Davie

Whether you're a first-time buyer or selling your old home to move up to something new, the buying and selling of a home is a big event. It's an intricate process involving many specialists. One of these specialists is a realtor, whose job it is to make the transfer of property as easy as possible.

That's why many buyers and sellers turn to a realtor. As a member of their local real estate board, realtors have their finger on the pulse of the housing market and are in daily contact with buyers potentially interested in your home.

You can trust a realtor to protect your interests and to look after details. And all the while, you're an active partner in the process, working with a realtor every step of the way. So the more you know about buying and selling homes, the better your working relationship with a realtor.

A realtor is knowledgeable about developments and trends in real estate. A realtor will get you the facts: comparable prices, neighborhood trends, housing market conditions and more.

BUYING A HOME:

Finding the perfect home doesn't happen in one day. There are a number of things you can do to simplify the process, including defining financial parameters, potential neighbourhoods and the desired features in your next home. Do you need an extra bathroom, a garage, a fenced backyard, or lower utility bills? Do you want a fireplace, a short drive to work, or maybe minimal yard work? Once your list is complete, decide what is most important to your lifestyle.

Location affects your day-to-day living and is one of the most significant influences on value. Your choice of location may be limited somewhat by the price you can afford. Even so, make sure you consider such things as distance to work, schools, shopping and entertainment.

What type of property do you want? A single-family detached home is attractive to many people because it typically provides more living space and land. On the other hand, a condominium may be a more appropriate choice for you, with an emphasis on maintenance-free living.

A realtor can help you analyze all of these buying issues. A realtor working as a buyer's agent works to find the connection between homes available in the market and the needs and financial capacity of buyers. Talk to and compare the services of realtors to help you navigate through this complicated business transaction. Be comfortable and confident with the realtor you are selecting as your business partner.

Once a realtor knows your needs, desired neighbourhoods and price range they can come up with a list of suitable properties available through the MLS system.

When you select a property and decide to visit a house, there are many things to consider. Does it have all the features you wanted? Is the neighbourhood what you expected? Try to picture your favorite furnishings in a room. Remember all of the technical considerations, such as type of wiring, power outlets, heating system, roof and foundation, and condition of windows, doors and plumbing.

Home inspection services are available for a reasonable fee and having a qualified home inspector look at the house is always a good idea. Generally speaking, the older the home, the greater the need for professional inspection.

Once you find the house you want to make your home, work with a realtor to develop an offer. In the offer, you should specify how much you're willing to pay. State when the offer expires, and suggest a closing date for the transaction. You can also propose some conditions on the offer. Some common types of conditions are:

getting a suitable mortgage (include the amount, interest rates and any other figures you feel important);
selling your current home (the seller may continue to look for a buyer, but will give you the right of first refusal);
the seller providing a current survey, or a "real property report," showing the location of the house on the property owned by the seller and that there are no encroachments;

- the seller having title to the property (your lawyer will check this out when he or she conducts a title search to see if there are any liens on the property, easements, rights of way or height restrictions);
- if there is a septic system, the seller should have a health inspection certificate, stating the system meets local standards;
- if you still have any doubts about the home's safety and construction, you may wish to make the purchase conditional on an inspection by a qualified engineer;
- any inclusions - basically, what stays and what goes.

You will need to present a deposit along with your offer. An appropriate deposit will show your good faith to the seller. The seller's agent is bound by law to bring all offers to the seller's attention.

After your offer is accepted and all the conditions are met, the offer becomes binding on both sides. If you walk away from the deal at that point, you may lose your deposit. You may also be sued for damages. Make sure you understand and agree with all of the terms of the offer before signing.

You'll also have to reimburse the seller for the unused portion of any prepaid property taxes or utility bills. As well, you must also pay any legal fees, and, if applicable, any realtor fees. Be prepared to furnish proof to your lender that you have insured your new house as well.

Before the property can formally change hands, there are still a few things to do. On or before closing day, your lawyer and the seller's lawyer will arrange to transfer title of the property from the seller to you. The mortgage money will be transferred to your lawyer's trust account, and then to the seller, and your lawyer will bill you all additional expenses such as land transfer taxes or outstanding legal fees.

At this time, be sure to check with your lawyer that everything is as stated in the offer-to-purchase. Once you're satisfied and the keys to the front door are in your hands, there's nothing else to say... except welcome home!

SELLING A HOME:

In today's market, many homeowners have considered "going it alone" and selling their homes without the help of a realtor to "save the commission." However, once they realize how complex and intimidating a real estate transaction can be, many people reconsider and enlist the services of a realtor. There are more than 145 steps to complete a real estate transaction. It requires an organized, step-by-step approach that many homeowners just don't have the time, skill or experience to carry out.

A realtor provides a variety of services including help in setting a listing price within current market guidelines. They develop a marketing plan, offer recommendations and advice to make your home more attractive and "saleable," and act on your behalf during negotiations to ensure your interests are protected.

Another advantage of working with a realtor is the far-reaching market exposure your home will receive through the Multiple Listing Service® (MLS®). This co-operative marketing system relays information about your home to a vast network of realtors and therefore, potential homebuyers in your market. The greater the exposure your home receives, the more likely you are to find a buyer willing to pay your price.

Selling your home is not a simple procedure. It involves large sums of money, stringent legal requirements and the potential for costly mistakes. A realtor is committed to spending the time it takes to help you sell your home in the least amount of time and for the best possible price.

A realtor must disclose to you in writing, who exactly they represent in any real estate deal. A realtor may represent a buyer or a seller; they may also represent both buyer and seller in the same transaction. Your listing realtor is, in law, your agent. An agent owes his or her client the duties of utmost care, integrity, confidentiality and loyalty. Make sure you discuss agency with your listing realtor.

The process of selling a home with a realtor starts with the Listing Agreement. It's a contract between you and the brokerage company that the agent represents. It is a framework for subsequent forms and negotiations. It's important the agreement accurately reflects your property details and clearly spells out the rights and obligations of all parties. Both you and the listing agent sign the listing agreement and each receive a copy. The agreement binds both parties to its terms and conditions.

Review your selling strategy regularly with your listing agent: Is your house being shown regularly? Are you receiving the feedback from prospective buyers? Are you in touch with the marketplace? Is your property competing well? If not, what else can you do?

Once a buyer is found, you'll be receiving an offer that will detail how much, specify any conditions that may apply or be attached by the buyer, say when the buyer would like to take possession, and when the offer expires. As an act of good faith, the buyer will make a deposit with the offer.

You don't have to accept the offer as is. You may wish to make a counter offer that comes part-way to meeting the offer's conditions. The counter offer is one more step along the way to negotiating the final terms and conditions of the sale. The offer, once signed by everyone, is a binding contract. Make sure you understand and agree to all of the terms in the document. You may want to have it reviewed by your lawyer before signing.

Before closing, especially if the buyer makes it a condition of sale, you may be asked to provide a current survey, or a "real property report," showing the location of the house is on the property owned by you and that there are no encroachments. You may also have to prove that you have title to the property (the buyer's lawyer will check this out when he or she conducts a title search to see if there are any liens on the property, easements, rights of way or height restrictions). Especially in rural areas, you may also be asked to provide a certificate for a well or septic system, stating the system meets local standards.

The buyer may also make the purchase conditional on an inspection by a qualified engineer or inspector.

Then on or before closing day, lawyers representing you and the buyer will set up a trust account for the money coming from the sale and will pay off any mortgages you owe on the property. After these are paid, you will receive any money you have coming from the sale.

You must deliver the property deed or transfer documents, mortgage details and keys to your lawyer. Your lawyer will register the mortgage discharge and transfer the deed at closing,

Your lawyer should also ensure that you receive compensation for prepaid expenses such as, property taxes, electrical or gas bills, or if applicable, any heating oil left in your tank. Some lenders will make it possible for your mortgage to be portable, so you can take your mortgage with you when you move to your new home.

Here, your responsibilities under the listing agreement end. You'll have paid your listing agent the agreed-upon compensation. This can be done by your lawyer who can arrange the payment from the proceeds of the sale. In some provinces, including Quebec, notaries perform the same role in the real estate transaction as lawyers do in other provinces. If you have any questions, check with a realtor.

The sale of property is a complex business transaction. There are distinct advantages to having a realtor who is well-educated, knowledgeable, and experienced. A realtor also has access to an array of services, including the Multiple Listing Service®, which can provide you with instant, thorough and accurate property information.

Some Keys to Home Ownership:

1. Pay off Debts: especially high-interest credit card debt. This will help you qualify for a mortgage and make your mortgage payments easier without other debts to pay.

2. Cut Unnecessary costs: For example, sell your vehicle and use public transit (or walk to work if it's close by). Put proceeds from sale of your vehicle towards a down payment on a home and save big on vehicle payments, insurance, repairs, license, plates and maintenance.

3. Reduce Rent Costs: Take in a roommate who will pay half the costs of rent, utilities etc., thereby allowing you to set aside money for a home purchase (if you and your partner are buying a home together, share an apartment to cut costs) Moving to a 1-bedroom or bachelor apartment can also cut costs or move back to your parents' home

4. Quit Smoking: Smokers who quit can also save thousands of dollars a year – and cutting back on alcohol consumption is also a cost-saver.

5. Take the Free Way: Enjoy Free shows / entertainment over costly paid shows – and go for other 'free' options such as borrowing library books instead of buying books.

6. Raise funds: Beyond cost-cutting, raise funds via freelance work, second job, etc.

7. Get Pre-Approved for a Mortgage: This will let you house hunt knowing how much you can spend and save time in arranging a mortgage.

8. Use a Realtor: Select a professional agent who is a good fit with you and your needs to offer expert assistance in making what is likely the largest transaction of your life.

Great Advice! / Michael B. Davie

Sources of Great Advice:

Edo Bergsma / www.remax.ca/on/edo-bergsma
A Knowledgeable Consumer is Our Best Customer

Edo Bergsma is an easy-to-talk-to, very knowledgeable, personable agent, who believes in looking out for the best interests of his clients and guiding them to smart decisions they'll be pleased with for years to come.

As an agent with RE/MAX Escarpment Realty Inc. he's part of a local powerhouse brokerage with over 500 realtors and offices throughout the Hamilton-Burlington area and premier market share in its trading area. Ranked #1 by the local Real Estate association every year since 1994, RE/MAX Escarpment also offers a network of mortgage brokers, insurance brokers and lawyers to answer your questions and service the remaining steps in the buying or selling process to ensure you get all the help you need to make your experience as smooth and successful as possible. Websites have also developed to maximize exposure for listings and customize the search process for buyers. With buyers moving to the area from all over the world, the brokerage is equipped to communicate in various languages to help clients feel more at home.

Edo's recent listings cover a wide area, from Ancaster to Toronto, Brant County, Burlington, Cambridge, Dundas, Flamborough, Glanbrook, Guelph, Eramosa, Haldimand County, East Hamilton, Hamilton East, Hamilton Mountain, Hamilton West, London, Norfolk County, Waterdown and West Lincoln.

Edo Bergsma at Re/Max Escarpment Realty Inc:
www.remax.ca/on/edo-bergsma / 519-647-2780
1595 Upper James Str. Unit 101, Hamilton, ON, L9B 0H7

Sources of Great Advice:

Judy Marsales Real Estate Ltd. / www.judymarsales.com
Excellence is our Minimum Standard

Since opening its doors in 1988, Judy Marsales Real Estate Ltd. has carved a special niche as one of the Hamilton area's few independently owned and operated real estate firms. Headed by Judy Marsales, a former member of Ontario Parliament who has also served as first woman president of the Metropolitan Hamilton Real Estate and as president of the Hamilton and District Chamber of Commerce, Judy Marsales Real Estate Ltd. has grown to more than 50 sales associates working out of three offices.

With a strong focus on the local community, the prosperous brokerage is proud of its truly talented, successful Real Estate Professionals, attributing its success to its clients and the people they work with. The Company has earned a reputation for exceptional client service, professionalism, strong business ethics and most importantly, performance. With 3 helpful Hamilton area offices to serve you:

Westdale Office:
986 King St W, Hamilton, ON L8S 4R5
Phone: (905) 522-3300 / Fax: 905-522-8985
Email: westdale@judymarsales.com

Ancaster Office:
253 Wilson St. East, Ancaster, ON, L9G 2B8
Phone: 905-648-6800 / Fax: 905-648-6848
Email: ancaster@judymarsales.com

Lock Street South Office:
263 Locke Street South, Hamilton, ON, L8P 4C2
Phone: 905-529-3304 / Fax: 905-529-3304
Email: locke@judymarsales.com

Great Advice! / Michael B. Davie

Sources of Great Advice:

Mortgage Financial Corp: / www.mfco.ca
Your Home. Your Life

Mortgage Financial Corporation, founded by Ken Lindsay in 1990, is today one of southern Ontario's largest independently owned brokerages. Just as an insurance broker finds you the best deal on insurance, a mortgage broker finds you the best deal on a mortgage.

They also deal with a vast number of lenders, all competing for your business. This means Mortgage Financial Corporation is working in your interest to find you the very best mortgage (rate, terms and flexibility) in today's market – and their clients come from all over Southern Ontario.

Due to the great referrals from their existing clients their service area continues to grow. People look for financing for various reason; home purchases, debt consolidations, commercial properties, loans and lines of credit, and the company's professional mortgage services are available to guide you through these difficult and possibly unfamiliar times to save money through proper debt management. Whether you are a first time buyer, doing a switch of an existing mortgage to a better mortgage rate or seeking a debt consolidation Mortgage Financial clients are spreading their name as the broker of choice for high quality service.

Ray Street, Hamilton Head Office:
Ken Lindsay, Mortgage Broker of Record
12 Ray Street South, Hamilton, Ontario. L8P 3V2
www.mfco.ca
(905) 529-2521. Toll Free Line: 1-866-604-8860.
Fax: (905) 525-9701.
Email: ken@mfco.ca

Great Advice! / Michael B. Davie

Chapter-Key 2:
Get a Good Job

It's time to start a Full-time job with enough income to support an independent lifestyle – with careful budgeting It may also be time to start a career – here's advice on how to go about choosing and building the career that's right for you, including getting the right credentials, good work habits and more:

Landing steady employment is a major accomplishment in today's work world where contract positions have replaced job security of the past.

With few exceptions, no longer can you reasonably expect to work for the same employer for the rest of your adult working life, retire with a good pension and enjoy a comfortable retirement.

Instead of landing a life-long job, you're more likely to move from one contract job to another in today's mobile employment environment.

Your now-possibly-required mobility may mean moving from contract employer to contract employer within the same city – or you could find yourself moving across the country – or both. It's something to keep in mind and prepare for as you survey the employment landscape.

Toronto-based Ryerson University states its graduates can expect to take on multiple roles in diverse industries - on average 15 jobs across three sectors over the course of your career for life, which now replaces a single job for life.

So, while you likely will not have one job for life, you will probably have a career for life comprised of many different jobs in your career field, with a variety of employers in different locations.

There is also a growing tendency for people to work well past the once-standard mid-60s retirement age to instead work well into their 70s. Long hours are very much the norm for many people.

All of this means it is more important than ever to choose a rewarding career path that you enjoy, that interests you, and fulfills you while providing you with sufficient income to finance a comfortable lifestyle and perhaps support a family as well.

After all, if you're going to spend more than half of your awake hours working, it's best that you like the work your doing and find it satisfying and rewarding. You don't want to spend the rest of your life doing work you dislike, dragging yourself to jobs you hate.

You need to take control of your life, choose a career with work you enjoy doing and build a good life for yourself and your loved ones.

It's been said that if you truly enjoy what you do, you'll never work a day in your life – and there's more than a grain of truth to that old saying, so set yourself on the path to enjoyable, satisfying, paid employment.

Great Advice! / Michael B. Davie

Ryerson advises that with job markets evolving at a faster speed and new sectors developing like never before (AirBnB, Uber, etc.), careers no longer evolve linearly. Throughout your career, you may choose to change jobs to develop new skills, gain further training, receive mentorship, secure a higher salary, or simply to embark on new challenges.

The university notes that students gain valuable experience testing out skillsets and preferences through volunteering and work experience gained through part-time jobs, internships or co-op. As a graduate and new professional, you will continue to grow your network and build what is now called your foundation career (years 10-15 after graduating). Then, moving into mid-career, you will be defining your professional self and as you discover what drives you, possibly alter career paths or pursue continuing education to strengthen your skill set.

Ryerson states that rather than retirement, professionals today are building legacy careers and working into their 70s as they explore and adapt their career to suit their lifestyle. As you embark on building your career for life, staying adaptable is essential. Identify and seize growth opportunities, and remember that your career for life is an exciting and continual learning process, encompassing educational, professional and personal growth.

If you are uncertain about your career direction, or who wish to explore viable options, and want to learn about resources available to help you make appropriate strategic decisions, career advising appointments are available with a Career Education Specialist at the Career & Co-op Centre.
(Ryerson University, 350 Victoria St, Toronto, ON M5B 2K3, 416-979-5000 www.ryerson.ca)

Your Job Search:

Yes, you can still visit your local employment offices and check the job boards for employment opportunities – but my own approach – one I recommend for you – is for you to first determine, which companies you'd like to work for, then go to their respective websites to check them out.

Chances are, if they have any positions available, they'll post these on their website along with detailed information on the skills, credentials and experience they're looking for in a job candidate.

You can often apply online and attach your resume to your application that is sent straight to the appropriate person screening candidates.

National employment websites also list jobs by job type and location with good descriptions – and I highly recommend visiting job websites such as workopolos.com and monster.ca (this is a Canadian website but there are similar such sites in the US, UK, Australia and elsewhere).

Networking should also be part of your job search. You may have friends or contacts who are already working for one or more of the companies you're interested in working for now or in the future.

Your contacts may know of upcoming job openings that haven't even been posted yet or have only been posted internally.

It certainly doesn't hut to have a conversation about potential employment opportunities.

Great Advice! / Michael B. Davie

Cover Letter and CV-Resume:

Your cover letter should be brief and to the point: You're applying for a specific job so it should state the job you're after and introduce yourself as a worthy job candidate.

You can provide some of your qualifications as well and state why you're best-suited for the job – but keep in mind you're also providing a CV-Resume with good details and you don't want there to be much overlapping of info.

Your cover letter should also convey a sense of who you are as a person so you stand out from the other candidates.

Your resume will need to be more detailed and more than your cover letter's few paragraphs. Ideally you'll get all of your qualifications, credentials, education and experience onto a single page with 1-inch margins top, bottom and sides. If you need more space to fit everything in, then a second page is acceptable – but don't go beyond two pages.

Keep in mind the company HR person or recruiter will be sorting through a massive stack of cover letters and resumes from job-seekers. Anything poorly worded or containing spelling or grammatical errors will be promptly rejected and tossed in the trash can to help whittle the pile down.

So, with that in mind, you'll want to make sure your cover letter and CV-Resume are free of spelling mistakes and grammatical errors – and that the information you're providing is well organized, clearly worded and well presented (key points in bullet form for easy readability etc.). All information should be clearly shown at a glance.

Use an easy to read respectable font and put a space between each paragraph so that the resume 'breathes' and looks balanced, not crowded. You can also refer to or even download resume templates online that you can customize for your own needs.

Your resume content should of course include your name and all contact information, including email, phone number and mailing address; along with your objective statement (why you want the job and are the best person for it) at the top of the page.

Also, list all prior jobs with descriptions of valuable skills in a bullet-pointed list – and do the same for your education credentials, listing programs and skills acquired, especially those relevant to the position sought.

When listing skills, also include so-called soft skills such as communication skills, conflict resolution abilities, team player, able to work well with others and on own initiative, etc. and include hobbies and interests at the end of your resume as these help to humanize you ands set you apart from the competition. It can also help if you list volunteer work helping worthy causes etc. to show you're responsible and caring and active in the community in a positive way.

When listing job titles you've had, include a brief description of your duties and skills – especially those most relevant to the position sought.

Try to quantify any positive outcomes you achieved at a prior employer. For example, if you improved the company website or brought a follow-up system to the sales team and your initiatives increased sales by 20% that's worth stating.

Improving your credentials:

Taking training courses or earning a certificate or degree in your chosen field is always a good idea, as is life-long learning. It adds to your knowledge base and know-how. It adds to your combination of accomplishments, skills, and education that help you stand out from others in your field and it increases your value to the prospective employer.

Be prepared for the Job Interview:

Here are job interview tips from thebalancecareers.com:

1. Practice and Prepare
Mentally go over typical job interview questions and prepare answers for them. Strong answers are those that are specific but concise, drawing on concrete examples that highlight your skills and back up your resume. Your answers should also emphasize the skills that are most important to the employer and relevant to the position. Be sure to review the job listing, make a list of the requirements, and match them to your experience.

Note that even the most well-prepared response will fall short if it doesn't answer the exact question you're asked. While it's important to familiarize yourself with best answers, it's equally important to listen carefully during your interview in order to ensure your responses give the interviewer the information they're looking for.

Also, have a list of your own questions to ask the employer. In most interviews, you'll be asked if you have any questions for the interviewer. It's important to have at least one or two questions prepared to demonstrate your interest in the organization. Otherwise, you might come across as apathetic, which is a major turnoff for hiring managers.

2. Develop a Connection with the Interviewer
In addition to indicating what you know about the company, you should also try to develop a connection with your interviewer. Know the interviewer's name, and use it during the job interview. (If you're not sure of the name, call and ask prior to the interview. And, listen very carefully during introductions. If you're prone to forgetting names, jot it down somewhere discreet, like in small letters at the bottom of your notepad.)

Ultimately, building rapport and making a personal connection with your interviewer can up your chances of getting hired. People tend to hire candidates they like and who seem to be a good fit for the company's culture.

3. Research the Company, and Show What You Know
Do your homework and research the employer and the industry, so you are ready for the interview question, "What do you know about this company?" If this question is not asked, you should try to demonstrate what you know about the company on your own.

You can do this by tying what you've learned about the company into your responses. For example, you might say, "I noticed that when you implemented a new software system last year, your customer satisfaction ratings improved dramatically. I am well-versed in the latest technologies from my experience with developing software at ABC, and appreciate a company who strives to be a leader in its industry."

You should be able to find out a lot of information about the company's history, mission and values, staff, culture, and recent successes on its website. If the company has a blog and a social media presence, they can be useful places to look, too.

4. Get Ready Ahead of Time

Don't wait until the last minute to pick out an interview outfit, print extra copies of your resume, or find a notepad and pen. Have one good interview outfit ready, so you can interview on short notice without having to worry about what to wear. When you have an interview lined up, get everything ready the night before.

Not only will planning out everything (from what shoes you will wear, to how you'll style your hair, to what time you will leave and how you'll get there) buy you time in the morning, it will also save you from having to make decisions, which means you can use that brain power for your interview.

Make sure your interview attire is neat, tidy, and appropriate for the type of firm you are interviewing with. Bring a nice portfolio with extra copies of your resume. Include a pen and paper for note-taking.

5. Be On Time (That Means Early)

Be on time for the interview. On time means five to ten minutes early. If need be, drive to the interview location ahead of time so you know exactly where you are going and how long it will take to get there. Take into account the time of your interview so you can adjust for local traffic patterns at that time. Give yourself a few extra minutes to visit the restroom, check your outfit, and calm your nerves.

6. Try to Stay Calm

During the job interview, try to relax and stay as calm as possible. Remember that your body language says as much about you as your answers to the questions. Proper preparation will allow you to exude confidence.

As you answer questions, maintain eye contact with the interviewer. Be sure to pay attention to the question so that you don't forget it, and listen to the entire question (using active listening) before you answer, so you know exactly what the interviewer is asking. Avoid cutting off the interviewer at all costs, especially when he or she is asking questions. If you need to take a moment to think about your answer, that's totally fine, and is a better option than starting out with multiple "ums" or "uhs."

7. Follow-Up After the Interview
Always follow up with a thank-you note reiterating your interest in the position. You can also include any details you may have forgotten to mention during your interview. If you interview with multiple people from the same company, send each one a personal note. Send your thank-you email within 24 hours of your interview.

According to the Experis Manpower Group:
Want to ace your next interview and land that open job you've been seeking? Here are 20 tips to help you prepare.

1. Research the industry and company.

An interviewer may ask how you perceive his company's position in its industry, who the firm's competitors are, what its competitive advantages are, and how it should best go forward. For this reason, avoid trying to thoroughly research a dozen different industries. Focus your job search on just a few industries instead.

2. Clarify your "selling points" and the reasons you want the job.

Prepare to go into every interview with three to five key

selling points in mind, such as what makes you the best candidate for the position. Have an example of each selling point prepared ("I have good communication skills. For example, I persuaded an entire group to ..."). And be prepared to tell the interviewer why you want that job – including what interests you about it, what rewards it offers that you find valuable, and what abilities it requires that you possess. If an interviewer doesn't think you're really, really interested in the job, he or she won't give you an offer – no matter how good you are!

3. Anticipate interviewer's concerns and reservations.

There are always more candidates for positions than there are openings. So interviewers look for ways to screen people out. Put yourself in their shoes and ask yourself why they might not want to hire you ("I don't have this," "I'm not that," etc.). Then prepare your defense: "I know you may be thinking that I might not be the best fit for this position because [their reservation]. But you should know that [reason the interviewer shouldn't be overly concerned]."

4. Prepare for common interview questions.

Every "how to interview" book has a list of a hundred or more "common interview questions." (You might wonder just how long those interviews are if there are that many common questions!) So how do you prepare? Pick any list and think about which questions you're most likely to encounter, given your age and status (about to graduate, looking for a summer internship). Then prepare your answers so you won't have to fumble for them during the actual interview.

5. Line up your questions for the interviewer.

Come to the interview with some intelligent questions for the interviewer that demonstrate your knowledge of the company as well as your serious intent. Interviewers always ask if you have any questions, and no matter what, you should have one or two ready. If you say, "No, not really," he or she may conclude that you're not all that interested in the job or the company. A good all-purpose question is, "If you could design the ideal candidate for this position from the ground up, what would he or she be like?"

If you're having a series of interviews with the same company, you can use some of your prepared questions with each person you meet (for example, "What do you think is the best thing about working here?" and "What kind of person would you most like to see fill this position?") Then, try to think of one or two others during each interview itself.

6. Practice, practice, practice.

It's one thing to come prepared with a mental answer to a question like, "Why should we hire you?" It's another challenge entirely to say it out loud in a confident and convincing way. The first time you try it, you'll sound garbled and confused, no matter how clear your thoughts are in your own mind! Do it another 10 times, and you'll sound a lot smoother and more articulate.

But you shouldn't do your practicing when you're "on stage" with a recruiter; rehearse before you go to the interview. The best way to rehearse? Get two friends and practice interviewing each other in a "round robin": one person acts as the observer and the "interviewee" gets feedback from both the observer and the "interviewer." Go

Great Advice! / Michael B. Davie

Chapter-Key 3:
Mine Your Own Business

Yes, that's <u>mine</u> your own business as a small business can be a virtual gold mine of extra wealth, extracting a secondary or even primary source of income while providing a strong source of satisfaction and enjoyment – truly a rewarding experience, but you need to do it right. More and more in these uncertain times, job security is an outdated notion. Having a secondary source of income via a business is a wise move – and if it grows enough to fully support you, why not seize the option of living your dream and being your own boss?

Starting your own small business puts you in the driver's seat, generates income and is likely one if the smartest moves you'll ever make – and it's surprisingly easy! It's also becoming something of a necessity for many.

In today's age of economic uncertainty, having your own small business can be an effective employment safeguard and a good source of primary or secondary income.

For most people, the era of secure jobs with benefits and pension plans is long over. Job security, once considered a commonplace certainty in the 1950s through 1970s became a rarity in the decades that followed and is today looked upon with a sense of nostalgia for the vast majority of employees. Things are different now, especially for those in the millennial generation, and for many in prior generations, including some baby boomers.

Today, it's common for jobs – even careers – to be based on a temporary contract or freelance position, void of benefits and with little job security of any kind.

For anyone facing a degree of employment uncertainty, starting your own business, even as a hobby, can provide a secondary source of income you can fall back on should your regular fulltime employment be interrupted or end.

So, take a careful thorough approach: Figure out what you want your business to do – perhaps building on a hobby or area of interest or a passion.

Next, explore the market for the product or service you've decided to offer and seek out potential customers - some online research will help you determine who and where your customers are, what they like and what product or service features are the most attractive to them.

Decide on your business model – determine if you want to incorporate or be a sole proprietor or form a partnership etc. Open a business bank account that also provides bank statements so you can track revenue and expenditures. Set up cash flow projections and develop your brand that sets you apart from competitors.

Minimize your start-up costs and try to self-finance at the start as much as possible. Set up a Business Plan outline in broad terms what your goals are and what you hope to achieve.

Join business oriented social media sites – LinkedIn is a favourite of mine – and promote yourself and what you have to offer on LinkedIn, Facebook, ReferralKey etc. via postings, event pages, setting up interest pages and groups, etc. Build your contacts list into the thousands and keep in touch via postings and invitations to events.

Starting a business can be the start to fulfilling a dream and living an independent lifestyle in which you are your own boss and you call the shots, set your own hours, give back to the community and much more. But there are also a lot of things you need to be aware of and watch out for – so let's get started with some great advice:

Depending on where you live in the world, there are likely business organizations such as chambers of commerce and/or boards of trade to provide expert advice.

While researching this book, we relied on such business organizations, particularly the Business Development Bank of Canada, a federal Crown corporation wholly owned by the Government of Canada. Its mandate is to help create and develop Canadian businesses via financing, growth and transition capital, venture capital and advisory services, with a focus on small to medium-sized enterprises.

Do you dream of being your own boss? Do you have a great idea for a product or service? Are you looking for a way to give back to your community and country? If so, then starting your own business might be the right choice for you.

We have lots of resources to help you assess whether you have the right personality to be an entrepreneur, explore business ideas and get started.

We help create and develop strong Canadian businesses through financing, advisory services and capital, with a focus on small and medium-sized enterprises. We support entrepreneurs in all industries and at all stages of development from 123 business centres across Canada and online at bdc.ca.

We're committed to the long-term success of Canadian entrepreneurs and we understand that a business is more than just dollars and cents.

We complement the role played by private-sector financial institutions and have been serving Canadian entrepreneurs since 1944.

We are a financially sustainable Crown corporation and we operate at arm's length from our sole shareholder, the Government of Canada.

Self-assessment
Starting a business can be a rewarding and enriching experience. However, it might not be the right professional choice for you. Before making the leap, take a few minutes to find out whether the opportunities and challenges of entrepreneurship fit with your personality.

Try our online entrepreneur self-assessment.

Explore ideas and ask questions
You may be loaded with talent and itching to get your company started, but it's important to take the time to think about how you will turn your idea into a successful business.

Is your idea original?
If you have a truly innovative idea, then you have to find out if it needs intellectual property protection to prevent it from being copied by others.
If your product or service isn't original, then ask yourself how you're going to go head-to-head with competitors.

How will you differentiate your offering?
How will you make money with your product or service?
While you may think your product or service is amazing, you still have to find out who your target customers are and what your source of revenue will be.

Questions that you need to answer include:
What is your target market?
How much are your target clients willing to pay for your products?
If your clients won't pay for your products or services, do you have an alternative business model?
How will your product or service be delivered to market?

Will you be developing, producing, packaging, marketing and distributing your product or service? Or will you partner with other companies to bring it to market?

For first-time entrepreneurs, it can be daunting to master these steps. That's why it might be best to start by focusing on the one thing that makes you stand out. You can then partner with other businesses to help you with non-core tasks.

You might, for example, choose to focus all your efforts on product design, but licence your product to a more established partner to manage its production and be responsible for marketing and distribution.

What resources do you need?
Once you've established what you're going to do and how you want to do it, you'll have to figure out how much it will cost.

You'll want to establish how many employees you'll need, your timeline to market launch as well as the one-time and recurrent costs you'll have to pay. Make sure to include expenses for things like office space, office supplies and various insurance and benefits in your estimate.

Once you've answered these questions, outline your estimated projected income for your first year. Base this estimate on the size of your market, industry trends and your expected market share.

After you've answered all these questions, you'll be well on your way to writing your first business plan, which you can use to attract investors and lenders.
Your business plan is a crucial document for your new company. It says who you are, describes your business and shows how you will become profitable.

A properly formulated plan can help you gain the confidence of lenders, investors and other stakeholders. As such, it should show you're committed to your business and have the skills, knowledge and confidence to achieve your goals.

The elements of a good business plan:
Your business plan should include the following elements:
Your company name and a description of your business
A market and competitor analysis
A discussion of what makes you different from the competition
A marketing plan
Your organizational and legal structure
An HR plan
An analysis of your financial and equipment needs
Your key financial data

BDC's article "How to write an effective business plan" provides a brief outline of the key elements of a plan. You can also read our article on common mistakes to avoid when building your business plan.

You can use BDC's free business plan template to guide you as you write your plan. The Canada Business Network also offers a guide to writing your business plan as well as good examples of industry specific business plans.

Obtain supporting information
You've probably already conducted informal market research on your own. But you'll need more than anecdotes to convince investors and lenders to support your business. Your business plan has to be backed by facts and research to hold up to scrutiny.
You should gather this information using both secondary and primary sources.

Secondary sources will consist of statistics and trends about your market and your customers. The websites of Statistics Canada and Innovation, Science and Economic Development Canada are good places to obtain this data.
Industry publications, associations, think tanks and university research are also good sources of information. Also consider contacting a Canada Business Network centre to see if they could help you find what you're looking for.

Primary sources include surveys, personal interviews and focus groups. These can provide you with insights into the attitudes and behaviours of your target customers. Make sure to survey more than your personal network of friends and family when conducting your research.

Like the rest of your business plan, your market research should be periodically reviewed and revisited anytime you need to make major business decisions.

Set measurable objectives
Setting goals for your business will help you to get your team focused and taking action to achieve your vision. Your goals can deal with every aspect of your business plan. Here are some examples:

Finance — Raise a specific amount of capital, hit cash flow targets, become profitable.
Operations — Launch new products, offer new services, improve efficiency by x amount.
Human resources — Find employees with specific skills, create an onboarding protocol, introduce an employee evaluation system.
Sales and Marketing — Create a unique brand, develop your marketing plan, set sales targets.

You should have measurable targets so you can monitor your progress towards them through the year.

Do you need a marketing plan?
If your business will rely heavily on marketing, you may want to create a separate marketing plan. For a general introduction to marketing concepts, consult BDC's article "A 5-step, no-nonsense marketing plan."

Your marketing plan can include the following elements:
A SWOT analysis that identifies your firm's strength's weaknesses, opportunities and threats.

A profile of your target market.

Clear objectives in terms of market share and segments, number of customers and customer retention, and the size and volume of purchases that are made.

A description of your marketing strategy.

Prepare an elevator pitch
Apart from your business plan, you should also prepare an elevator pitch. This is a short and compelling description of your business that can be delivered in 60 to 90 seconds.

The idea is that not everyone will have the time to or be interested in reading your business plan. To elicit their interest, you need to be able to pitch potential investors, lenders, partners and customers on your business in the time it takes for an elevator to go up a building.

To be successful, your pitch needs to be clear and concise, stand out from the crowd and be tailored to your audience. You'll also need to know your business inside out, as listeners may come back to you with difficult questions.

With your business plan in hand and a clear idea of where your company is heading, you now have to determine what structure your business will take, decide on a name and choose where your business will be located.

Select a company structure
The first thing you'll want to do is determine what business structure best meets your needs. The structure you choose will in large part depend on whether you are running the business by yourself or together with partners.

There are four different business structures in Canada:

1. Sole proprietorships

This is the simplest form a business can take. It offers relatively low start-up costs and few regulations. But be aware that you are personally responsible for all debts and obligations your business incurs.

2. Partnerships
In a partnership, each partner shares the profits and obligations of the business. This type of business structure requires a partners/shareholders agreement.

3. Corporations
A legal entity entailing more regulations, corporations have higher start-up costs. The advantage is that shareholders have limited responsibility for the debts and obligations of the company.

4. Co-operatives
A corporation controlled by its members.

Choose a business name
Choosing a name may prove more difficult than you'd expect. Your name must be accurate, catchy and, most importantly, available. Finding the right name can almost be a science — there are even companies who specialize in providing this service.

When you register your company, a search is typically done on the Canadian trade-marks database. Finding a unique name may be extremely difficult, or as simple as adding your initials or rearranging the words slightly.

You do not need to register your company or choose a name if you plan to operate under your own name and are using your personal bank account — as a consultant, for example. But you will need to apply for a GST or HST number if you earn more than $30,000 a year.

Register your business (and get a business number)
A number of provinces require businesses to register for provincial tax regimes. Visit the Canada Business Network site for additional information on registration across Canada.

If you are incorporating, you must decide whether to incorporate provincially (if you plan to do most of your business within your province) or federally (good for protecting your company name across Canada).

When you register your business, you will obtain a business number, which will help you file your taxes and hire employees, among other things.

You can apply for a business number online. Depending on your province, you may be able to register for provincial programs at the same time.

Do you need to protect your ideas or inventions? Learn about patents (for inventions), trademarks (for words, symbols, designs) or copyrights (for created works). The Canadian Intellectual Property Office offers more information and several searchable databases.

Set up shop
If you are renting space, you will probably have to sign a commercial lease. You may want to consult your lawyer to understand all the clauses in the lease before signing it.

Whether renting or buying your premises, you will need insurance to protect your assets. Most banks will suggest an insurance broker, but it can pay to shop around yourself.

Maybe you're still planning your business or you've just started it. Whatever the stage, you have high hopes for your company. You want it to grow.

As you know, success is far from guaranteed. Starting a business is risky. That's why many financial institutions shy away from lending to start-up businesses.

So, you'll want to look at different sources of financing such as venture capital and the one I most recommend, self-financing via your own personal investment in which you decide on the amount to be invested and the timeframe to made that happen. Self-financing can usually be done slowly over time so you can recoup your investment.

Strategic Planning:

A strategic plan is your road map to the future. It's a coordinated and systematic way to develop a direction for your company, determining where your organization is going over the next few years and how it's going to get there.

It includes an executive summary (usually written at the end of this exercise); company description, mission-vision-values statements strategic analysis outlining strengths, weaknesses, opportunities and threats. It also includes an action plan setting out business strategies, budget and evaluation methods plus objectives and a description of what your company is all about and the value accorded it.

Strategic planning will help you to see failures as temporary set-backs you can learn from and use to improve your business while focusing on your short and long-term goals with an action-oriented approach.

Great Advice! / Michael B. Davie

Stopping your inner Self-destructive Saboteurs

Beyond any financial constraints, a fledgling entrepreneur can also be hit with self-sabotage as they come to second-guess themselves and become consumed with self-doubt as their self-confidence vanishes to be replaced by debilitating fear of failure, fear of acting on your dreams.

This was very much the experience of fellow Manor House author Paula Hope, who learned to overcome her inner demons and write the insightful book ***Stop The Saboteurs – Conquer Negative Thoughts that Hurt Your Revenue and Your Brand.***

As Paula recounts in this excerpt from her book: "In retrospect, I realize I had been bored, truly bored, with the routine of my role as an executive. My work had become soulless. I was losing my *joie de vivre*. I was "of a certain age," and my personal responsibilities had diminished somewhat. I had worked forever to support others. I was living in dangerous times for my own selfhood and it was time. Time to move on to the life that I really wanted. Where I could do what I loved and let the money follow, find my bliss and live happily ever after. I could experience the zen of working from my own creativity and be rewarded for my courage by unimaginable wealth. I knew that having my own consulting business was what I wanted. I could do it. I had lots to offer and I was going to get out there and grab it all by the tail."

"I was brimming with conviction, passion, and experience and, of course, confidence. Except I wasn't. Brimming with confidence that is. Not only was I not full of confidence, I was missing a lot of it. In fact, I had none left."

"I realized that I was terrified," Paula recalls. "Terrified of *actually* living by my own wits and doing what I had always dreamed of doing."

"How could this be?" she asks. "What the devil was getting in my way? Overnight, I had realized the true, private hell of the professional service provider. The one that can take over your soul when you suddenly become your own brand. Everything that I said or did became the object of public scrutiny. Even more serious and debilitating was the fact that everything I said or did became the object of my *own* scrutiny. And I was bitterly unhappy with what I saw in myself."

"The sickening feeling in the pit of my stomach was an experience that I thought was totally of my own making. It sounds strange now, but I felt isolated and alone every time that dread would visit me … until I saw that same terror on the drawn faces of my fellow entrepreneurs. They talked too much, too, and muddled their way through — just like me! They were scared, too!

"I discovered that I was not alone in my despair as a professional service provider. There were many others who were terrified by the responsibility of generating their own revenue. They were overwhelmed by the realization that, "If it is to be, it is up to me."

"Learning more about coaching allowed me to admit to my own fears, and it became easier to recognize those fears in others as I encountered people in my own network. I began to study the emotions within myself and others with a morbid fascination. I eventually could give a name to these wretched feelings that occur when transition conspires with the sudden "you are the brand" reality — it can create a full-blown identity crisis. I named these horrible beings, these embodied fears **"The Saboteurs."**

Paula notes such "saboteurs" can often include second-guessing and doubting your own abilities via self-limiting beliefs; procrastination that causes you to miss opportunities and harbouring a "scarcity mindset" in which you have an ungenerous attitude towards yourself and others, that can include not giving out referrals in the mistaken belief that helping others limits your own success when in fact sharing referrals builds trust and relationships and fosters a business environment of abundance.

Although referrals can be an enormous source of business opportunities, Paula notes negative thoughts about public networking – referral saboteurs – can also play havoc. She notes:

"This Referral Saboteur highlights the pathway by which a simple personality trait, being an introvert, is hyperbolized into a reason for not attending networking events and not developing networking or referral-building skills. Introverts represent more than 50 per cent of the world's population and networking is the most powerful method for creating new business. Does it make sense for introverts to deny themselves the opportunity to create the revenue that they deserve due to a perceived weakness of their personality make-up? A Referral Saboteur, indeed, is at play here," she notes.

"A very common, and quite lethal, Referral Saboteur is lurking in the statement, "I am an introvert; therefore, I can't be effective at networking." This Referral Saboteur assumes that there is some type of magic or mystery to revenue generation. This thought pattern suggests that only business professionals with special powers and personalities can be "rainmakers" and find their ideal clients. Unfortunately, "I'm an Introvert" is yet another very dangerous Referral Saboteur." She adds.

Creating Success
The biggest challenge to creating success in your business, by far, lies in conquering or managing the Saboteurs. Isolating, addressing and expunging *as many* negative thoughts as possible is the real key to your success.

Negative thoughts, or Saboteurs, as the coaching world and I call them, hold all of us back from the life we deserve. These self-doubts, second thoughts and undermining voices in our own heads are responsible for many of life's losses… whether it is Olympic podiums, sports teams, companies, organizations, families or individuals, it is the quality of the thoughts between the ears of the participants that best determines successful outcomes.

We hear about this principle of the power of thoughts in many places now. PMA, the acronym for positive mental attitude, is an example of this approach. If we are positive, we will attract positive results and avoid the problems that could so easily derail our efforts. And it is true. From the many pundits who have brought us *The Secret*, or PMA, to my first moment with this concept when I studied Pirandello's play entitled *Right You Are Who You Think You Are* in university, we have learned that positive thinking is very powerful — and very effective.

Over the last several decades, an entire self-help industry has emerged to assist us with managing our thoughts. This important and fascinating field generates about $11 billion yearly in North America, creating entirely new approaches to management, leadership, coaching (in and out of the sports world) and many other areas of human activity in its wake. And we are fortunate, deeply fortunate, to have access to this positive-thinking philosophy and psychology.

The challenge is that positive thinking, for all its beauty and ready accessibility, cannot embed itself into anyone's thoughts if there is a lot of background noise. That noise is the unique mix of those potentially 40,000 -50,000 negative thoughts in every individual. The inner squabbling by the Saboteurs becomes a cacophony of fear and doubt that can paralyze the thought-holder for life and litter their world with difficulties — if they do not address these thoughts or self-limiting beliefs.

Self-limiting beliefs, negative thoughts that become "truths" to the individuals who are harbouring them, can embed themselves from the time we are unsuspecting children. These negative thoughts burrow into the unconscious mind, where they are held and fed until their owners come to believe them, even if they are entirely irrational. Intellectually, people may reject the concept that they have embraced emotionally, creating boatloads of internal confusion.

Winning with the Saboteurs
As my knowledge of training and coaching business professionals in referral marketing strategies developed over the years, I came to understand the role of the Saboteurs in preventing worthy business professionals from creating the revenue and the success that they deserved.

I also came to appreciate the power of education in the eradication and prevention of the Saboteurs. When business professionals are properly trained and coached in the three skill sets that they require to grow their business or practice by referral, the Saboteurs have no place in their lives. They cannot find a foothold in a business professional's subconscious mind as their revenue grows and they attract more and better-quality referrals. Creating relationships for the pocketbook and soul feels magnificent!

I realized that if business professionals could manage their Saboteurs through coaching, training and ongoing reinforcement, they were going to be successful, as long as they maintained a routine that supported their networking and referral-building activities.

Seven Steps to Create Revenue for Business professionals:
1. Isolate, address, manage or expunge all Saboteurs.
2. Take good care of yourself.
3. Set the correct intentions (goal setting) and feel the emotions of victory.
4. Embrace lifelong learning about new business development as the primary strategy for protecting your revenue.
5. Learn about the attitudes and skills that lead to success, including networking, referral-building and sales-closing strategies.
6. Develop a system for your new business development activities that includes daily, weekly, monthly, quarterly and yearly plans. Commit to ongoing reinforcement through training and coaching until you wind down your business and no longer require the revenue. Be open to change.
7. Oh yes, and enjoy the ride. Create a routine of new business development activities that you can embrace, working with people that you like, and who appreciate you as you like and appreciate them. Leave room for unexpected opportunities. The Booked Solid Referral Marketing Plan© helps you play more and work less, while growing your revenue joyfully.

Want to Stop the Saboteurs?

- Invite Paula to energize and inspire your group by going to www.bookedsolid.ca/speaking or calling 905-483-0355.

- Explore Booked Solid Programs for ways your organization can move forward – go to www.bookedsolid.ca/onsite or call 905-483-0355

- Have a look at Booked Solid online programs – they have helped countless others just like you to succeed – go to www.bookedsolid.ca/homestudy

- Consider Coaching with Paula – go to www.booksolid.ca/coaching to explore your options and see whether working with Paula is right for you

- Sample the Monday Morning Referral Tips – go to www.bookedsolid.ca/referraltips

The Booked Solid Programs for Saboteur Antidote and Saboteur Prevention are designed to help you get serious about your Saboteurs. *Now.* These programs have helped countless others free themselves from self-sabotage and create the revenue that they deserve.

Sources of Great Advice:
Paula Hope / Booked Solid: www.bookedsolid.ca
Create the Revenue You Deserve

Paula Hope helps business professionals create the revenue they deserve. She speaks, writes, trains and coaches business professionals to conquer their Saboteurs by growing their networking, referral-building and sales process skills. She is a leading expert on referral marketing and strategic networking, owning her own business, aptly named "Booked Solid".

During her 30-plus-year sales and marketing career, Paula has developed her sales wisdom and compassion for those on the front lines of new business development.

With *Stop The Saboteurs*, her first book, Paula applies decades of expert experience to offer solutions towards conquering the self-destructive fears and self-limitations that can impede success. This breakthrough book provides invaluable advice previously only available to her many clients, for whom she has worked wonders in helping them overcome negative thoughts to turn failure into triumph.

As Paula notes: "At Booked Solid, we uncover all of the next steps to grow your revenue by growing your referral, networking and sales closing skills – *and Stop the Saboteurs forever!"*

Booked Solid, Oakville Head Office:
Paula Hope, President/CEO
101-2275 Upper Middle Road East, Oakville, ON L6H 0C3
www.bookedsolid.ca (905) 483-0355 paula@bookedsolid.ca

Sources of Great Advice:
Business Development Bank of Canada: www.bdc.ca
We're committed to the long-term success of Canadian entrepreneurs and we understand that a business is more than just dollars and cents.

The BDC (Business Development Bank of Canada) is a federal Crown corporation wholly owned by the Government of Canada. Its mandate is to help create and develop Canadian businesses via financing, growth and transition capital, venture capital and advisory services, with a focus on small to medium-sized enterprises.

Do you dream of being your own boss? Do you have a great idea for a product or service? Are you looking for a way to give back to your community and country? If so, then starting your own business might be the right choice for you.

The BDC helps create and develop strong Canadian businesses through financing, advisory services and capital, with a focus on small and medium-sized enterprises. We support entrepreneurs in all industries and at all stages of development from 123 business centres across Canada and online at bdc.ca.

With 2,200 employees and $28-Billion in assets, the BDC complements the role of private-sector financial institutions and has served Canadian entrepreneurs since 1944.

BDC Montreal head Office:
Michael Denham, President/CEO
Address: 123 offices in communities across Canada
www.bdc.ca   1-877-232-2269   social@bdc.ca

Great Advice! / Michael B. Davie

Great Advice! / Michael B. Davie

Chapter-Key 4:
Build Your Brand with Marketing

It's time to start a Full-time job with enough income to support an independent lifestyle – with careful budgeting It may also be time to start a career – here's advice on how to go about choosing and building the career that's right for you, including getting the right credentials, good work habits and more:

Even before you start a business, you should have a sense of your market and demand for the goods and/or services you'll offer. Once you have the business up and running for a few months, a marketing plan is a vital means to exploit your market, bring in revenue and make your business grow. Here's what you need to know to set up a marketing plan tailor-made for your business now and in the future.

The importance of effective marketing cannot be over-emphasized: The old story that immediately comes to mind concerns the failed businessmen who didn't believe in advertising and never took out an ad – until the day he took out an ad advising he was going out of business.

Fellow Manor House author Susan Crossman is an expert marketer, successful writer-editor and head of Crossman Communications, who understands the success-building effectiveness of marketing. She's also the author of the critically acclaimed **Content Marketing Made Easy – Why You Need it / How to Do It**, a book that's a virtual bible of terrific advice. I highly recommend you get this remarkable book via Amazon, where it hit Number One in its genre category within weeks of its release, and continues to provide key marketing advice to grateful entrepreneurs.

I can't begin to cover the wealth of information Susan shares in **Content Marketing Made Easy – Why You Need it / How to Do It**, but I'll share a sample of her wisdom via the following excerpts borrowed from her book:

"Online marketing can be intimidating, no doubt about it," Susan notes, "and I spend my days simplifying it for business people so they can generate more revenue as a result of their online activities."

Susan adds: "The businesses my team and I help tend to have a few things in common":

- They know they need to improve their online marketing efforts but they just don't know how to get started.

- They suspect they might be losing out on customers that have actually been finding their competitors online instead of them.

- Some of them have attended an online marketing course or workshop and decided that content marketing was the "wave of the present." They became excited about the possibilities — but then went back to their businesses and the project went nowhere. (And, if that's you, I bet you're feeling pretty frustrated because you KNOW that this is important but you just haven't had the time, energy or knowledge to make it happen.)

- They might have started to develop an online marketing strategy at one point but it was a lot of work and it was confusing and they let the project slide in favour of easier, more important tasks.

- If they already have an online content marketing program they're now looking for new distinctions that will help them become more effective so they can increase their client base and grow their business.

- Or, finally, sometimes they've decided to improve their online marketing efforts and they know they need to do it, but their area of brilliance is not marketing and they realize they could really use some help and advice on how to make this happen.

"Does any of that sound familiar?" Susan asks. "Whatever your reasons are for exploring content marketing in more detail, please take heart. Although there are countless distinctions that can be made in this exciting field it is a process that can be taught, learned and duplicated. Once you have a program up and running, it's a straightforward way to generate more business as long as you're willing to cultivate your results with a fair bit of consistency. It takes time."

"We are moving towards a world where a huge percentage of business is done online and if you are not playing in that field, eventually you aren't going to have a business. Pretending these changes aren't happening won't make them go away. And, while there still seems to be a place for direct mail in our marketing mix, and there is definitely a role for networking, I believe that developing and polishing our online content is the key to the kingdom," she adds.

"Content marketing is an effective way to differentiate our businesses in the marketplace, while helping our perfect clients get to know, like and trust us," Susan explains. "Most business people like to make money. Most of us would also like to make more money than we are currently generating. Let's face it, the effort required to build and run a successful business is huge. If we can find a way to streamline the process so that we can reach more people with less effort — and a moderate investment — wouldn't we want to do that?"

Content marketing is all about informing people without working too hard at selling them. The theory is that if you provide lots of valuable information you will show people that you are awfully good at what you do and lead them to a state where they know, like and trust you so much that they simply want to do business with you. The more ways you can find to do this, the bigger an online profile you can develop, and the more your business shines. If you do this well, you will make it obvious to anyone looking for the service you provide that you are the ONLY choice.

I don't believe that content marketing can replace personal networking for a service-based business. You still want face-to-face opportunities to meet people and develop ways for them to get to know you and what you do. And there are many other strategies for marketing your business digitally. But your online content management strategy is a great way to support any other marketing you do. People might meet you at a networking event but if they are remotely interested in doing business with you they are going to search you out online.

Your content drives your online rankings and the more organized and effective you are in developing your content, the more people know about you and the more you can grow your audience. You don't have to do it all at once, but you do need to get started. Is waiting until next month, next quarter, or next year — when you understand it better, or when you have "fewer other priorities"— going to benefit your business? There is no time like the present to get started.

So what can content marketing do for your business? Your online content marketing strategy gives you a bigger online footprint than you, as a small business, might otherwise generate. It should also:

- Allow people to find out more about you

- Help people see what working with you is like

- Show your target audiences who you are and what you can do

- Help educate people about how to improve their own businesses or lives

- Tell people that you are available as experts in your field and

- Increase your credibility

What's fun for me in working with my clients is watching their online garden grow – it takes time and effort but it's ultimately extremely satisfying.

Content is something that's been around for decades and so has marketing, and it's a good bet that telling a good story online is going to remain one of the most powerful ways to differentiate your business in a competitive market and give your potential customers good reason to do business with you. There is nothing magic about content marketing. But the results can be magical.

Marketing is the process of starting conversations with the people who know they want what you are selling. The conversations themselves are what sales is about. So marketing starts the conversations that the salespeople handle.

You might start those conversations today at a networking event or a trade show. You might start those conversations by handing out brochures, business cards, newsletters or key chains. You might also start those conversations through your website, Twitter feed, Google + page or your blog. There are unlimited opportunities out there for starting conversations with people. But you want to make sure that you put your time, money and energy into starting your conversations primarily with people who might want what you are selling.

So, what is content marketing?

Content marketing is about creating a substantial body of content related to your business and the needs of your ideal clients and sharing it through online platforms such as your website and your Linked In, Facebook, Twitter, You Tube and Google+ profiles. You want the content to tell your company story authentically so that it generates trust, credibility and likeability for you, and calls upon your viewers and visitors to take another step in a growing relationship with you.

Your online content is informational rather than blatantly "sales-y." And it has at its heart a respect for potential clients, acknowledging that they might want to some research before they engage in a conversation with a potential supplier. It builds trust and authority for you amongst your ideal customers and it supports your relationship with them. Providing helpful online content positions you as a valuable resource for people who need what you provide."

If you do this well, human visitors and search engines will reward your efforts and you will generate greater revenue as a result.

Did you know that some statistics estimate that 80% of all business transacted involves the internet in some fashion? And that up to 80% of business decision makers prefer to get company information in a series of articles rather than an advertisement? Many people report in surveys that content marketing makes them feel closer to the sponsoring company, and, that company content helps them to make better product decisions.

Susan notes that Red Bull is an energy drink company that runs something called the Red Bull Content Pool. It stocks more than 50,000 photos and 5,000 videos about sports, culture and lifestyle.

Although Red Bull is a large corporation with enormous amounts of money to throw at their content marketing strategy, you can get involved with content marketing, too, to the limit that your budget will allow. And the more ways you can find to do this, the bigger the profile you can develop, and the more you can stand out in a crowd of other people offering what you offer.

If you do this well, you will make it obvious to anyone looking for the product or service you provide that you are the ONLY choice in the field and your competition will fade into the background by comparison. And you will generate more revenue as a result.

Susan recommends you consider reaching and expanding your audience and customer base via regular blogging, emailing out a company newsletter, updating your website with new content, utilizing videos and reaching out to the media and public via press releases and social media promoting the goods and services you offer, but in a manner that shares helpful information and builds trust and confidence. She notes that companies that blog tend to generate 67% more leads than companies that don't blog and that more than half of marketers have found customers via social media sites such as LinkedIn and Facebook. She also notes that all of this content marketing is in addition to your regular marketing efforts.

"Your own unique process of making a sale still stands. It's just that your content marketing efforts will give your prospects more opportunities to get to know more about your company and what it can do for them. It supports your sales team and any other marketing you do," she notes.

Networking for Success

Content marketing is clearly important to your success – but that doesn't mean it's time to stop meeting people face-to-face. In fact, networking is another key component for most successful small businesses.

And your local chamber of commerce offers a wealth of opportunities to network and cultivate contacts, customers and suppliers.

 Achieving business success in the Hamilton market is made much easier and is accomplished in a more efficient manner through business community networking, an area that the Hamilton chamber and chambers of commerce throughout the world specialize in.

Great Advice! / Michael B. Davie

Clearly, businesses serious about success rely on a key organization for help: the Hamilton Chamber of Commerce. Indeed, the Chamber's slogan: "Creating Business Opportunities," speaks to the services it's provided for more than 170 years.

Chamber-created business opportunities include frequent chances to network: Members are provided with a number of catered business forums – most of them free of charge – throughout the year to promote their goods and services to 1,700 fellow Chamber members.

But the opportunities don't end there: The benefits are extensive – what you get out of the Chamber depends, in part, in what you happen to put into it. There are numerous breakfast meetings, special events and committees you can get involved with, and your involvement can bring you a good deal of insight and information on a range of topics.

Each chamber member has an individual reason for joining the organization so the chamber attempts to respond to those needs as individually as possible. The mission of the Chamber as the voice of ethical enterprise is that it is committed to making Hamilton a great place to live, work, play and invest, while recognizing the importance of the individual as the most significant contributor to achieving community objectives.

Indeed, the chamber's ongoing success is pegged to its central role in fostering the growth of Hamilton's traditional role as a major commercial centre. From very early in its history, before steel and heavy industry, Hamilton was a thriving centre of trade and commerce – a proud heritage that continues through to this day.

A Continuing History Benefiting Business Growth:

In 1845 – a year before the Hamilton community was duly incorporated as the City of Hamilton – the bustling community had by then established the Hamilton Board of Trade, the business-promoting forerunner of today's Hamilton Chamber of Commerce. And the importance of business people in making a difference wasn't lost on the board's first-ever president, Isaac Buchanan, a visionary who noted back in 1845 "without the committed leadership of those who strive to build an economy, our community will cease to strengthen and grow."

As well, the Hamilton Board of Trade had been an early supporter of free trade with the United States, although it reversed that position in 1910 to an effort to protect Hamilton manufacturers. Almost 80 years later the chamber would again support free trade with the Americans, indeed the world at large – an early pro-business initiative.

In 1903, the board pushed for civic improvements such as additional drinking fountains. It also formed an alliance with Hamilton's Trades and Labour Council to arbitrate an end to a costly Teamsters strike hurting the local economy.

And in 1920 another milestone was reached when the board reconstituted itself as the Hamilton Chamber of Commerce and quickly took on such successful projects as relocating McMaster University from Toronto to Hamilton and helping establish the Chedoke Golf Course.

During the Great Depression of the 1930s, the chamber showed compassion for the less fortunate members of Hamilton society. The chamber initiated a system of garden plots allowing the unemployed to grow produce. And it raised funds to cover rent owed by needy citizens.

Great Advice! / Michael B. Davie

From 1939-1945, the chamber supported the Second World War effort by organizing massive donations of foodstuffs and gifts for the City of Hamilton Tiger Squadron, a bomber squadron manned by local volunteers fighting overseas.

As Hamilton celebrated its centennial in 1946, the chamber played its usual active role, promoting, among other major events, the first Miss Canada Pageant.

During the 1980s, the chamber could be found supporting the Corporate Challenge fitness and fun event, Crime Stoppers and a Chinese chamber to attract Asian investment.

In the 1990s, the chamber continued its active role, speaking out on tax issues, government budgets and legislative concerns while bringing a lengthy list of prominent business leaders and speakers to the city to address everything from business strategies for success to exports and international trade.

During the 1996 Hamilton Sesquicentennial year, the chamber contributed enormously to making it a very successful year. Among the Chamber's many achievements was the introduction of a striking commemorative Sesquicentennial coin created by Ancaster sculptor Elizabeth Holbrook.

Also in the mid-1990s, the Globe & Mail's Report on Business magazine ranked the Hamilton area as one of the best communities in which one can do business in Canada. Clearly the Hamilton Chamber's oft-said message – that Hamilton is a great place to do business – seems to finally be getting out to the national media.

The need to repeat this message to wider audiences has been taken to heart by the chamber's many members who play a leadership role in building our economic region.

And this historic role is now being championed by a new generation of chamber members, many of them young entrepreneurs and small business people.

The chamber has experienced first-hand the rise of small businesses as the Canadian economy's leading source of new jobs and opportunities.

As the economy of Hamilton continued to evolve, an overwhelming number of chamber members are small businesses – and this continues to be the case. As entrepreneurs and small businesses now account for the bulk of new jobs and economic growth. At one time the major industries accounted for the bulk of jobs, but that's changed. Small businesses are now where you'll find the most employment growth. There are more small businesses around today than ever before – and that's certainly reflected in the chamber's membership – a trend that started in the mid-1990s and has continues to this day.

The mid-1990s was also when the chamber began targeting small businesses by starting programs that catered to one-man outfits to small firms with 100 or fewer employees.

Most of the growth in manufacturing jobs has occurred outside the steel industry via an abundance of small manufacturers each employing fewer than 100 people, including growth in services in general, high tech industries, bio-technology jobs and information services, and entrepreneurs are creating many of these new jobs. People getting into business on their own are creating their own job plus additional jobs for other people.

Great Advice! / Michael B. Davie

Small businesses, including home-based businesses, now constitute the fastest growing source of members at the chamber and this has led the organization to devote more time and energy representing the concerns of small business. That change in approach reflects a societal reality: Small businesses dominate the new age economy.

And by 2002, following the amalgamation of Hamilton and Wentworth as the single City of Hamilton, the total population exceeded 500,000 people – all of them residing in the now expanded city. Hamilton was a full-fledged metropolis of more than half-a-million people – and growing fast. Add in the interdependent, interconnected regions of Halton and Niagara and it's apparent Hamilton is the economic and geographic hub of an economic region of more than 1 million people.

The chamber is now focusing on how Hamilton can best take advantage of its enviable position at the hub of one of North America's most densely populated international markets. Within a 500-mile radius of Hamilton, about a day's truck drive, is a total market population of 120 million people.

The information age economy is also bringing new job opportunities. Fibre optic wire firms have made the downtown core a leader among inner city cores for its ability to offer high-speed Internet even in old buildings. This growth has also meant hundreds of jobs.

Efforts are also underway to develop Hamilton's 'smart community' potential, via uplinks to satellite linkages, allowing doctors many miles apart to have a fibre optic consultation on television screens. A diagnosis or patient information can be shared instantly via multimedia, telecommunication uplink technology.

The community has become a well-organized whole with once-distant institutions regularly conferring with each other to devise programs that can best exploit the new commercial and employment opportunities a changing business world is offering. The Chamber is in regular contact with the Hamilton Economic Development Department, Mohawk College, McMaster University and HIT (Hamilton Incubator for Technology), which serves as an incubator for start-up high-tech firms.

Demand for Skilled Trades:

Like many communities Hamilton is faced with shortages of skilled labour. Anyone with marketable skills – particularly skilled trades people such as tool and die makers, electricians, carpenters and machinists - are finding it relatively easy to find work.

The demand for new skilled trades people is there – the supply isn't, so Mohawk College is offering programs to create the needed skills. It's unfortunate that some firms are losing business because they lack skilled trades people and the jobs are going begging. The Ontario-wide shortage of skilled trades presents a huge opportunity for those people willing to learn a trade.

Chambers of commerce both develop and encourage business growth within an entrepreneurial culture – and they should be a key part of your business approach. The networking events and marketing opportunities to expand your business are among the many benefits you can reap.

Great Advice! / Michael B. Davie

Sources of Great Advice:

Susan Crossman / Crossman Communications**:**
www.bookedsolid.ca
I believe that developing and polishing our online content is the key to the kingdom

Veteran writer and author **Susan Crossman** is a speaker, editor and content marketing consultant, who helps Awakening Authors share the stories they are here to tell in powerful and inspirational ways.

Her expert book coaching and editing guidance helps her clients gather and organize their ideas and insights; structure their manuscript; express exactly what they want to say; and, get set up to publish and market their book, taking it from idea to printed reality.

Crossman Communications also mobilizes your business stories to enhance your brand through social engagement, digital content creation and inbound marketing initiatives.

The world of online marketing can seem technical and overwhelming but she's poised to help demystify the subject for you and develop a content marketing program that will help you increase sales, audience engagement, and customer retention: "We'll help you inspire your audience to take action that serves their needs while supporting your online goals, via websites, videos, social media, blogs, media kits, brochures, emails, and content to express your value proposition. Feeling overwhelmed? We'll take you from bewildered to unburdened – just schedule a free call."

Crossman Communications, Oakville Head Office:
905-469-1892 / Susan@CrossmanCommunications.com
www.crossmancommunications.com

Sources of Great Advice:

Hamilton Chamber of Commerce: www.bookedsolid.ca
Creating Business Opportunities since 1845

Created in 1845 by Isaac Buchanan and other merchants the Hamilton Chamber of Commerce is Canada's third oldest chamber, and Hamilton's oldest institution. It's dedicated to its members' success and offers these services:

1. Save you money via affinity programs only Chamber members can access. For small business, there is no better health and dental plan in the entire country to buy into. You can also get discounts on gas, office supplies, furniture and a whole lot more.
2. Facilitating commerce by building ties within the membership and hosting regular networking events. As connectors, we help you find the right lead.
3. Take political action by identifying priorities and developing policy with input from our members. The Chamber holds discussions with government to increase commerce and economic development.
4. Promote Hamilton and local businesses through a variety of local, regional and national media outlets, and our website, publications and social media to strengthen the local economy.
5. Provide solutions. If you need a key introduction, help dealing with government red tape or local market intelligence, we act as a lifeline and partner.

Hamilton Chamber of Commerce:
120 King St. W. Hamilton ON, L8P 4V2 (Jackson Square)
Phone: (905) 522-1151
E-Mail: hdcc@hamiltonchamber.on.ca
Web: www.hamiltonchamber.on.ca

Chapter-Key 5:
Live Healthy

Your health is of paramount importance – yet it's often overshadowed by financial or social concerns. But little else matters if you don't have your health. Here are great tips on healthy affordable diets and good eating, sleeping and exercise habits to make you strong and healthy and fit throughout your whole life and ready to take on each day with vigour and enthusiasm.

A healthy lifestyle is an absolutely crucial key component of your successful life. Your health is of paramount importance – yet it's often overshadowed by financial or social concerns. But little else matters if you don't have your health.

Picture yourself finally achieving financial growth or other life goals only to be derailed by health issues that forcibly shift your focus from achieving success to instead getting through a health problem – while everything else is put on hold. That's a costly counter-productive scenario that hurts.

But it can happen to the best of us – you're so caught up in your day-to-day life of working and paying bills, that you neglect your health – and perhaps don't even have a regular family doctor and dentist arranged.

Great Advice! / Michael B. Davie

I can still vividly recall my own horror story: I was in Washington DC covering a weekend international steel trade conference for *The Hamilton Spectator*. I'd was just completing filing the last of my trade stories electronically via my laptop computer prior to catching a flight home.

While typing away, I was chewing some sticky toffee that gripped and pulled out a dental filling, suddenly exposing the nerve of the tooth to air and moisture. In a split-second, I went from feeling fine to experiencing extreme throbbing pain on the one side of my face right up to the eye socket.

I called my dentist, arranged an emergency Sunday visit, caught my flight and went straight from the airport to his office where quickly replaced the filling, ending the pain.

Fortunately, I had previously established our family dentist, which meant the needed medical records and x-rays were all available – and my dentist himself was available, as he was making a special trip to his workplace on a weekend to see to the painful emergency of a longstanding client and friend.

I can't imagine how much longer and excruciating my ordeal would have been if I had also needed to find a dentist, get medical records transferred etc. all while coping with a great deal of pain.

Part of establishing your personal care program is ensuring you have adequate coverage. Health care varies by jurisdiction depending on what is publicly provided in whatever province or state or region in the world you reside in, so check what is available to you regarding public health insurance and then look into and select whatever additional private or company coverage desired.

In my own case, as a resident of Ontario, I get OHIP coverage and the Ontario Health Insurance Plan covers a wide array of medical costs, excluding certain unlisted things such as dental care, eye exams etc.

When working for corporate employers, I always enrolled in the company plan to ensure my family and I received care beyond that offered by OHIP.

After becoming self-employed, I selected a private plan – Benecaid – covering any prescribed drugs, dental and other care not covered by OHIP. You'll need to do a bit of online research to ensure you select the care options that are best for you.

Regular dental and medical check-ups are a must to keep on top of your personal health situation and address any issues that might exist with prompt treatment, to nip any problems in the bud before they grow into big problems.

But something often happens when young people head out to make their own way in life: The sensible healthy diet their parents' subjected them to is suddenly replaced by pizza and beer and junk-food; late nights and little time for medical and dental check-ups.

It's the start of an unhealthy lifestyle that diminishes energy, drive, alertness and potential for success in life.

This situation can also occur later in life especially if you're something of a workaholic putting in long hours and giving little thought to eating well balanced nutritious meals. Some retirees may also slack off on ensuring they get a proper diet in the mistaken belief this no longer applies to them as they're not actively in the workforce – but a healthy diet is important at any age.

Great Advice! / Michael B. Davie

Here are great tips on healthy affordable diets and good eating, sleeping and exercise habits to make you strong and healthy and fit throughout life and ready to take on each day with vigour.

Health Canada guidelines recommend a balanced diet following Canada's Food Guide (easily found online) with a daily serving of fresh, frozen or canned vegetables (free of added sugar or salt); plus a serving of leafy vegetables, fruit and juice.

For grains, whole grain bread rather than white bread is recommended along with cooked rice, pasta and cereal. All grain products should be low in sugar, fat and salt.

A glass of milk is recommended along with yogurt and cheese. Meat or alternatives can include cooked fish, shellfish, poultry or lean meat.

Or, you can turn to meat alternatives such as cooked legumes, tofu, eggs or peanut butter or shelled nuts. Use only small amounts of oil when cooking and this should be vegetable oil.

Also recommended: Drinking water as a calorie-free way to quench your thirst. Sugary deserts are out – in fact desert is not recommended, especially if you need to keep your weight and body fat down to healthy levels.

Exercise is also essential for good health. There are a number of reputable fitness clubs you can check out, along with aerobics and yoga classes. If you're at a desk for long hours each day and find you can't find the time to get out to a class to get and stay fit, you should have an at-home exercise program you follow.

Regardless of any fitness efforts, you should at least get up from your desk fairly frequently throughout the day and walk around. Walking is one of the best exercises there is.

You can also park your car at the far end of the lot so you walk farther to get to it – and whenever possible, go for long walks – great for your heart and respiratory system, and it's a low-impact healthy and frankly enjoyable thing to do for yourself. If you can go for walks with a spouse or friends, that too is a pleasant and healthy way to spend time together.

The key is to get yourself off the couch or away from your desk and start moving your body – you'll better because of it and will also be able to focus more effectively and generally enjoy life more.

Sleep is also crucial for good health. You need seven to eight hours of full sleep to feel rested to feel well.

Not enough sleep can understandably leave you feeling groggy, irritable and unable to properly focus. This in turn results in low-productivity, mistakes, mood swings and difficulties problem solving.

Severe sleep deprivation can lead to black-outs, hallucinations, comprehension problems, symptoms of psychosis and inability to properly perform routine tasks, including properly driving a motor vehicle.

So, make sure you get a good night's sleep every night, to ensure you start your day feeling rested, refreshed and mentally alert, ready to take on with confidence and good spirit, despite whatever challenges the new day may present to you.

Great Advice! / Michael B. Davie

"Without good health, you really have nothing," notes dentist Dr. Roland Estrabillo.

Dr. Estrabilllo also notes there can be a tendency for many people forego or eliminate altogether medical and dental check-ups and treatment. The predictable negative results include the likelihood of small, ignored problems becoming major health issues that can hamper and/or diminish the ability to function in a workplace or education environment.

Sometimes the practice of foregoing health care stems from a sense of false economy – time and money are initially "saved" by avoiding the doctor and dentist – but the end costs of treating the more serious ailments that inevitably develop usually exceed any initial "gain."

Nor does proper health care have to drain a modest budget: Most employers offer dental benefits and even when a paid benefits plan is not available, diligent, daily brushing and dental care along with regular inexpensive check-ups help you maintain dental health and avoid the need for treatment.

Dr. Estrabillo, who originally hails from the Philippines, has also established a charitable free clinic, as part of the Global Smiles International agency he started, that is providing dental care to Hamilton's impoverished citizens who cannot afford such services.

One Saturday each month, Dr. Estrabillo and volunteers from his staff of around 50 dentists, hygienists, dental assistants and support staff, freely give of their time and dental skills to help treat more than 400 patients at the free clinic annually.

"It's our way of giving back to the community and it's really incredible how generous our people are with their time," he explains in an interview at his Ancaster offices, where the free clinics also take place. "We see twenty people or more at each clinic and the services we provide range from hundreds to as high as a thousand dollars with all fees waived."

"We're coming from a place of generosity and many of the patients are very appreciative and grateful for this care," Dr. Estrabillo says of his Global Smiles International free clinics. "It's very satisfying to see the look on the patients' faces and to hear such positive comments."

Follow-up care, also at minimal cost to the patient, is provided at the dental hygiene school Dr. Estrabillo established in the lower level of the Ancaster building. The school, fully registered with the Ontario Ministry of Colleges and Universities and in the process of receiving formal accreditation, has become an important source of dental education and practical field experience.

The Sprawling Ancaster building also houses the dental hygiene training school and a dental lab.

For all of his patients, Dr. Estrabillo employs many of the latest technological advancements to make dental procedures as fast, efficient and comfortable as possible. He's also a life-long student who continues to learn from his mentors: fellow dentists, staff and friends from all walks of life who have helped him overcome problems and achieve new levels of success in his demanding career.

"Success is never something you achieve all by yourself. It's when learn from others and share your own experiences that you improve in the process. And everyone benefits from this type of sharing," he notes.

A teenaged Roland Estrabillo arrived in Canada from the Philippines in 1980. He was 19 and his arrival in The True North, Strong and Free, was the realization of a long-held dream.

"When I got here I just breathed in the air and looked around me and I knew anything was possible – I knew nothing could stop me from accomplishing anything I set out to do," he recollects.

"Every Canadian has the opportunity to pursue anything they want to do. We are so truly fortunate here, it's unbelievable. It really is the land of opportunity."

On arrival, it was found that he was lacking calculus, so he redid Grade 13 at St. Thomas Moore and then enrolled at the University of Toronto where he studied natural sciences for the next two years while pursuing a career in medicine.

Roland Estrabillo continued to pursue his medical studies, working summers and earning scholarships.

He was then ready for the next fateful step. Roland Estrabillo decided he would apply to the faculties of both medicine and dentistry and was accepted for both.

He turned to a friend, a professor in the faculty of nuclear medicine, who promptly asked the young man if he ever wanted to have a family and lead a normal life.

"I said yes," Dr. Estrabillo recalls, "and he told me to try dentistry, then come back after one year."

Roland Estrabillo took one year of dentistry studies and still wasn't convinced. So he took another "and I knew then that I'd found what I was looking for."

"I'm very grateful for having been steered in this direction and even my own children are very interested in following me and becoming dentists when they grow up. They've seen what dentistry is all about and they know it's a very worthwhile profession."

After Estrabillo graduated in 1987 from the University of Toronto with a degree in dentistry, he returned to Hamilton that same year to set up practice on Upper Wentworth Street, in a little 1,500-square-foot location next to a supermarket in a strip mall opposite Lime Ridge Mall.

As the youthful dentist began building his fledgling practice, he displayed a voracious appetite for information and ideas, boldly seeking out new ways of doing things, new ways of approaching dentistry and life in general.

This openness to new ideas and to learning from the success of others would have a profound and last effect on him.

As Dr. Estrabillo continued to evolve as a successful dentist and explored all that life had to offer, a pivotal moment would occur in 1989 while he was enjoying the splendour of islands in the Pacific Ocean.

The young dentist was wading into a warm water lagoon when a group of boisterous dolphins came splashing towards him, leaping through the water with unbridled joy.

As Dr. Roland Estrabillo stood transfixed in the water off a beach in Hawaii, the dolphins danced into the sheltered cove, chattering excitedly. They seemed to be beckoning the Hamilton dentist to join them.

"They have such a joyful attitude – wouldn't it be nice if you could be as happy as a dolphin in life?" Dr. Estrabillo adds, "and I love their sense of freedom, confidence and happiness. It was an experience I'll never forget."

Inspired by the dolphins, Dr. Estrabillo placed likenesses of their happy images on his business cards and practice literature.

As well, he's decorated the walls of one dental practice location with large illustrations of dolphins at play.

He's also infused himself and his staff with a contagious dolphin-like, happy, confident attitude that puts patients at ease and makes trips to the dentist more enjoyable.

"I still love dolphins," Estrabillo admits.

"The dolphin's image has become my own private signature – my patients are always bringing me little figurines and pictures of dolphins when they return from travelling. It's nice that people associate me with such a free and happy creature."

That Dr. Estrabillo would learn from dolphins and apply those lessons to his practice isn't surprising: He is determined to keep up in the rapidly evolving field of dentistry.

Dr. Estrabillo believes in lifelong learning and has long selected mentors from dentistry and other fields to give him guidance.

He also mainly uses porcelain, limiting his use of metals to gold and titanium – and only for special applications where porcelain is not the most appropriate material to use. He favours porcelain as it is durable, free of metals, and very natural looking.

And, he invests in computer equipment; technology, methodologies and materials to ensure his busy practice can treat his many patients fast and efficiently.

For example, although he now regularly makes use of an anaesthesiologist, the I-V sedation certification he earned a few years ago means that he can, if need be, comfortably sedate his patients for longer periods while he performs cosmetic dentistry or full-mouth reconstructive surgery.

It's this constant attention to the needs and concerns of his patients that have helped this dentist's practice achieve remarkable ongoing growth through a steady stream of referrals.

Back in the early 1990s, while building his practice from scratch, Dr. Estrabillo outgrew his mall location within his first few years of running his dental practice.

In the fall of 1992, Dr. Estrabillo moved his practice to renovated offices at his former home, just a little further north on Upper Wentworth Street.

But it wouldn't be long before he was again feeling cramped.

After expanding the number of operating rooms – known as operatories in the dental profession – to seven from four, he soon again found himself short of space.

Although general family dentistry still accounted for 60 per cent of his practice in the mid-1990s, Dr. Estrabillo was concentrating more on full-mouth reconstructive dentistry as a growing, satisfying, part of his work.

And by the late 1990s, Estrabillo was even more heavily involved in personally performing the more complicated dental procedures and "more surgery and less drill-and-fill work," while his practice as a whole continued to perform general dentistry.

"We work as a team – for example, after the orthodontist and periodontist have treated the patient, I perform bridge work, teeth implants, crowns, veneers and cosmetic improvements to teeth," he explains.

"We've cut the time needed for a crown to half an hour from an hour, so the patient is more comfortable."

Dr. Estrabillo now takes three hours instead of seven to perform most full-mouth reconstruction procedures.

He notes this dentistry can improve chewing efficiency, improve the functioning of the jaw, save teeth and "actually make people look younger with whiter, rearranged, straighter teeth which support the mouth better."

Both Hamilton locations are needed to keep pace with a burgeoning patient load that has now expanded to more than 12,000 patients on file.

Fuelling this impressive growth are referrals from satisfied patients who appreciate the extra care Estrabillo takes to make visits pleasant and brief.

Also fuelling referrals are the many services he can offer, including laser dentistry, whitening, and implant dentistry. "A lot of people come to us for a whole range of services, including teeth implants – and we like to help them get their mouths back in great shape," Dr. Estrabillo smiles.

Few people can combine the words 'dental' and 'exciting' in one sentence and make it work. But Dr. Estrabillo is very convincing when he confides: "It's just so exciting to be able to provide all these dental services to our patients – and it's very gratifying when you can help so many people."

Dr. Estrabillo clearly loves dentistry, and he's always looking for new ways of expanding his knowledge and skills in all dental matters.

Dr. Estrabillo is clearly putting his added time to productive use: In addition to a thriving dental practice, keeping current with the latest dental techniques, lecturing on matters dental and devoting attention to his family, he continues to learn from other successful people.

"I'm still into mentoring," he confirms. "It's a good learning process to talk to people who have achieved success in their lives and learn from them."

And he's grateful for the input, advice and support he's received from his mentors, fellow dentists, staff and friends from all walks of life who have helped him overcome problems and achieve new levels of success in a demanding, time-consuming career.

Sources of Great Advice:

Roland Estrabillo / Estrabillo and Associates:
www.ancasterdentalcare.ca
"Without good health, you really have nothing."

Dr. Roland Estrabillo directly attributes much of the success of his busy practice to his staff of 40 professionals, including hygienists, restorative hygienists (who can perform fillings work), support staff, and dentist associates. "My staff is great," he says with a grin. "Without them I couldn't succeed. We do the best job."

"We work as a team – for example, after the orthodontist and periodontist have treated the patient, I perform bridge work, teeth implants, crowns, veneers and cosmetic improvements to teeth," he explains.

"We've cut the time needed for a crown to half an hour from an hour, so the patient is more comfortable."

Dr. Estrabillo now takes three hours instead of seven to perform most full-mouth reconstruction procedures.

He notes this dentistry can improve chewing efficiency, improve the functioning of the jaw, save teeth and "actually make people look younger with whiter, rearranged, straighter teeth which support the mouth better."

Contact Information for Dr. Roland Estrabillo:
Phone: 905-387-2600 or 905-304-6300 Fax: 905-304-4768
Address: Hamilton location: 860 Upper Wentworth Street, Hamilton, Ontario, L9A 4W4.
Address: Ancaster location: 201 Wilson Street, Ancaster, Ontario. Email: dr.rolandestrabillo@drestrabillo.com

Chapter-Key 6:
Further Your Education:

Education has long been an established key to personal success, to achieving a good-paying job and-or career. It's particularly important to decide what you want to do in life and select the courses that will give you the knowledge and credentials to help you pursue your dream. Beyond the positive contribution of education on your job, career and income stream, furthering your education provides the less tangible benefits of helping you to grow as a person, develop analytical skills, learn to view things from different perspectives and much more. Your further education should be a matter of life-long learning as you expand your understanding of your life and the world around you.

Furthering your education is truly your ticket to a more rewarding life, both financially and spiritually. It's a move you'll really want to make to achieve greater success in your life.

A number of studies have shown higher education ultimately means larger pay cheques and wealth. Studies also show college and-or university grads tend to be happier and more satisfied with their lives – possibly in part because they're making more money.

And if the cost of higher education is deterring you – cast that concern aside. While the costs can be substantial including the repayment of student loans, these total costs pale in comparison to the cost of years of loss of income from not having a college and-or university education.

A 2013 Pew Research Center report (latest data currently available) surveyed and grouped Millennials generation full-time employees ages 25 to 32 by the highest level of education attained (Source: Pew Research Center survey, Oct. 7-27, 2013). The study made following observations:

1. High school grads had average annual earnings of $28,000 with 12.2% unemployed and 21.8% living in poverty. As well, only 40% were married and 18% were still living at their parents' home.

2. Those with a 2-year college diploma or at least some college education, enjoyed higher annual income – averaging $30,000 – that's $2,000 a year more than those who had graduated high school but not gone beyond that. The percentage of college Millennials unemployed was just 8.1% - nearly a third less than the 12.2% high school group's rate. The college poverty rate at 14.7% was also about a third lower. Slightly more were married at 41% and slightly fewer were living with their parents at 16%.

3. The most dramatic results were in the most-educated group: Millennials with a Bachelor of Arts (BA) degree (or more). Average annual income for this group at $45,500 was more than 50% greater than the college group average. The unemployed percentage at just 3.8% was less than half the 8.1% college group's rate and less than a third the 12.2% high school group's rate. The University group also had the highest married rate at 45% and the lowest percentage still living at their parents' home – just 12% or two-thirds the 18% rate for the high school grads group.

The comparative results speak volumes: The most educated group enjoyed far greater income, and far lower

unemployment and poverty. They were also more likely to be married and not living at their parents' home.
Pew recorded similar findings for earlier generations such as the Baby Boomers and Generation X: Higher levels of education mean higher wages, lower unemployment and far less likelihood of ever experiencing poverty.

The Pew survey recorded the highest levels of job-career satisfaction belonged to those in the most-educated group, regardless of the generation they belong to.

Perhaps not surprisingly, this group, far more than the less-educated groups, tended to attribute-credit their education for being useful in preparing them for a job or career, indicating they owed some measure of their employment success to their education.

As well, the study found the vast majority of college-university grads - 88-92% - in every generational group state their education is or will be worth the investment in time and money.

Indeed, the costs of NOT getting a college and/or university education appear to exceed the costs of such higher education. Not getting such higher education often means not getting high-paying jobs, and over time the difference in income is far greater than the cost of higher education.

The benefits of higher education also appear to go beyond matters of income. Studies have also indicated the college-university grads are generally happier and healthier overall, exercising more and smoking less than less educated people. Grads also tend to do more volunteer work and vote more, taking a more active role in their community – these are generalities that don't apply to everyone, but they do appear to apply to the majority of grads versus non-grads.

It's certainly a strong indication that higher education is a path to a wealthier, happier and more active and satisfying-fulfilling life.

Simply put, higher education means higher income (in most cases – a degree in an obscure subject with no commercial application likely won't convey wealth unless perhaps you're the professor teaching it). It can also encourage a happier, healthier life.

Further Education and Lifelong Learning:

Improving your education is not something reserved for the young. Older students are becoming commonplace everywhere.

As mentioned, the advice in this book applies to various stages of life – if you're middle-aged or older, furthering your education is a smart thing to do – and you'll likely enjoy the experience as well.

For mature students, many programs offer credits for past or current life experience gained through employment for example that can help fast-track completing a program.

You may find getting that degree or diploma or certificate takes less time than you thought because of earned credits for life experience or other informal qualifications.

Whether you're getting that high school diploma, taking courses specific to a particular job or line of work; earning via an apprenticeship or simply taking interest courses, further education and lifelong learning will help you get more out of life.

Great Advice! / Michael B. Davie

I was in my mid-twenties when I studied and graduated with a Broadcast Journalism diploma from Mohawk College, one of the highest-ranked colleges in Canada.

Later, while in my late 30s early 40s I was a mature student at one of Canada's highest-ranked universities – McMaster University – where I earned degrees in Political Science during evenings while also working as a fulltime journalist with The Hamilton Spectator.

The degrees I earned helped me advance my journalism career with editor positions at larger newspapers The Globe & Mail and The Toronto Star.

Both Mohawk and McMaster are in my Hamilton hometown – and I would highly recommend them as both have track records of excellence and offer hundreds of courses in an array of fields taught by experts.

The diploma or degrees you earn at these institutions will help you life a better life with greater learning and employment opportunities.

I'd also highly recommend staying close to home when selecting an institution of higher learning as this reduces costs significantly and keeps you close to family and friends and perhaps your employer as well.

Further my education while staying close to home is an affordable option I'm very glad I took, an option I'd recommend for you as well - provided you have such an institution nearby and can get the courses you need-want of course.

You need to first decide what field-job-career you want to pursue, what courses or programs are needed to get you to where you want to be, and which colleges and-or universities offer these needed courses and programs.

If you can find what you need reasonably close to home – that's terrific. If you have to move to another city or commute, you'll need to weight the costs and pros and cons of making such a move.

There may also be the option of taking your desired courses online – but be careful and make sure the courses and programs offered online are legitimate, taught through recognized colleges or universities with good reputations and that the diploma or degree you earn is also recognized by educational institutions and employers alike.

Before making any decision, research online the various educational institutions websites and explore the descriptions of the various courses and programs offered.

You should also talk to program counselors by phone and in a face-to-face visit to gain insight into the education direction you're interested in taking. Read the course materials and reading lists to get a better idea of course content.

Take a Tour:

Once you've narrowed down your choices, be sure to arrange in-person visits with pre-arranged tours of the campus so you can get a sense of what life will be like for a few years as this will become something of a second home for you.

As courses and programs offered are often similar from one place to higher learning to another, you may want to favour the one with the best reputation for excellence in your chosen field.

Check out the School Culture:

Your own personality can be a lesser factor – all other things being equal, if you happen to have a liberal and or artistic bent, you may prefer a school known for its openness and diversity, innovation, creativity and 'liberal' culture.

If you happen to be more conservative in nature, you may prefer a school with more conservative values – but again this is all secondary to larger concerns of program content, teachers, location and costs.

Costs, grades, education history:

Check out the costs involved and admission criteria as these can vary widely between various schools. Costs can also be defrayed via student loans and-or grants so this should be explored as well via career-guidance counselors.

You'll also need to provide a transcript of your high school grades as par of the admissions process and if you think you can get credit for on-the-job skills you've learned and-or other such life experience, be sure to mention this in details as well. Most schools publicly post their admission criteria for the various programs offered.

When considering courses and programs look at all of the associated enrollment criteria – and consider your own criteria as well to ensure a good fit. You'll also want to look into offered work-study programs, counseling, health services and social-entertainment offered by each school.

Whatever you do to further your education should ultimately help you live a wealthier, more satisfying life.

Great Advice! / Michael B. Davie

Sources of Great Advice:

Mohawk College of Applied Arts & Technology
www.mohawkcollege.ca
Discover our wide selection of Certificates, Diplomas, Degrees and Apprenticeships

'Mohawk College educates and serves more than 31,700 full-time, part-time and apprenticeship students at three campuses in Hamilton, Ontario. Mohawk has been named one of Canada's greenest employers for five years in a row and is home to the country's largest net zero energy institutional building. Mohawk is also among the leading colleges in Canada for applied research, with a focus on sustainable energy generation and distribution, additive manufacturing and mobile and electronic health solutions.'

Programs include Business; Health, Communication Arts; Community Services; Graduate Studies; Preparatory Studies, Skilled Trades; and Technology courses.

Take the steps towards joining an in-demand workforce. Studying Skilled Trades or Apprenticeship at Mohawk means you will be training for a career within a booming industry at one of Ontario's largest colleges… Want to learn how to take the business world by storm? Our Business programs give you the knowledge, skills, and experience you need for a successful career in accounting, marketing, human resources, public relations, international business and more!

Contact Information for Mohawk College:
Phone: 905-575-1212 or 905-574-2600
135 Fennell Ave W, Hamilton, ON L9C 0E5.
Email: ask-us@ontariocolleges.ca

Great Advice! / Michael B. Davie

Sources of Great Advice:
McMaster University   www.mcmaster.ca
Canada's most research-intensive university
Committed to Creating a Brighter World

Founded in 1887, McMaster University is committed to discovery and learning in teaching, research and scholarship and has a student population of 23,000.

Bringing together the best and brightest minds is the spark that makes a Brighter World possible.

At McMaster, we measure our success by the degree to which we improve people's lives, contribute to our global knowledge base and advance the societies in which we live. Learn about the groundbreaking research taking place at McMaster, the people behind it, and the positive impact of our discoveries.

As well, the DeGroote School of Business delivers education with purpose. We actively foster interdisciplinary thinking and evidence-based management to transform business and society.

The DeGroote difference is that you'll be challenged to apply your knowledge to practical business situations, gaining an understanding of how the concepts you're learning today will impact the business world tomorrow.

Contact Information for McMaster University:
Phone: 905-525-9140
Address: 1280 Main Street West, Hamilton, ON L8S 4L8
Website: www.mcmaster.ca

Chapter-Key 7
Nurture Your Relationships

Building happy, loving relationships is what life is all about. Financial success means little if our relationship with our self and others is rooted in unhappiness. After all, what is the point of achieving career success and accumulating wealth if our core being is ill at ease, if our home is a place of tension and animosity. We need to find joy and fulfillment within ourselves and through our relationships with others. It's vitally important that our relationships be based on good communication coupled with realistic expectations and a willingness to work things out, so that we share a calm, successful state of serenity.

Fellow Manor-House author Samantha Cervino discusses unrealistic and potentially harmful societal expectations in her breakthrough book **The Dragonfly Effect – Finding Your Inner Strength, Clarity and Wisdom**. She notes:

"In our search for true love we may go through life stumbling through unsuccessful relationships. We may put ourselves in situations that leave us not only broken-hearted but also filled with self-doubt and fear that maybe we are not worthy of this ideal life and relationship we desire…"

"From a young age we believe in everlasting love at first sight as depicted in fairytales and movies. We grow up with the idea that our life will turn out just like the characters' lives in fairytales. We're all Cinderella and all men are Prince Charming. As little girls we dream of our wedding day, wearing that beautiful white wedding gown, with our prince waiting for us at the altar…"

As Samantha notes, these unrealistic expectations come at a high price: "As we all know, a wedding can be pretty expensive and before we even say "I Do," anxiety and stress start to build up. Without realizing it, this is how we start our married life, with stress about money."

"Our husband-to-be may not tell us about his stress about all this planning and spending, only because he loves us and does not want to hurt our feelings. So, he stays quiet and does as he is told. Does this sound fair to him? Is this fair to us? We are now entering into a marriage and relationship where there is no open trust in communication because we are afraid of being misunderstood. And whether we are able to acknowledge this or not this affects our marriage from that instant on. I feel this needs to be discussed and the pressure taken off..." she adds

"Let me remind us all that Cinderella is a fairytale and I myself bought into that as well. Do not forget the real reason why you are getting married in the first place. Be patient with one another. You are going from being on your own to sharing a home with someone. That's a big change and it's very exciting."

As Samantha points out, it's important to learn to love yourself and make your relationship with yourself work so you can then love others from a position of strength and confidence: "When I finally had enough with my life the way it had been for years, I made a decision to change things *for me*. I would look at myself in the mirror and see pain in my eyes, always hiding behind an empty smile. I felt deep inside that I was more than what I was seeing reflected in the mirror. I knew I was denying myself freedom, happiness and love. This was spirit telling me to get out of my own way and start loving myself and respecting myself. What a new concept that was for me, to respect myself and to love me, to accept me with all my beautiful imperfections..."

Ultimately, as Samantha concludes, it all means reaching a healthy balance in your life: "What does it mean to live a well-balanced life? It means to live a life in which you are at peace with yourself. You have money-freedom, time-freedom, you are in harmony with the universal laws."

Healing and Nurturing Relationships

Every relationship has its rough patches that need to be resolved so that the relationship can get back on track to the benefit of both parties.

To better navigate such problem areas, I turned to fellow Manor House author Rebecca Rosenblat, registered psychotherapist and couple's counsellor, and author of **Overcoming Betrayal – The Breakthrough Therapeutic Approach: A couples Guide to Healing from Both Perspectives**.

Here's her advice on healing relationships via finding detours rather that risk everything through confrontations:

"The journey is definitely worth it, hard as it may feel at times. To make it bearable, keep in mind that *life is about finding detours, versus becoming defeated by roadblocks; and journeying together is a whole lot easier than flying solo*!

And here is a list of tips to aid understanding and healing:

Rebecca's Top Tips:
- Every story has two sides – it's foolish to make decisions without hearing each other out. Healing happens when we understand and support each other.
- Each side needs to own their stuff, to avoid feeling like a victim, and to control their future.
- Understanding each other's pain is the fastest way to recovery.
- People *can* change, if they're fully invested in it. But change in response to pain or pressure often disappears as those factors disappear; change in perspective can last forever.
- Our childhoods impact us more than we realize, because we learn to do relationships based on what we experienced growing up. So any healing work has to involve family of origin issues.
- Those whose parents were reliable, learned to cope with their misfortunes; those who had unreliable parents didn't develop healthy coping skills.
- Those who could trust their parents, can let others in; those who couldn't trust them, don't feel safe enough to let others in.
- If you think someone else is more compatible than your partner, compare your family histories to see if that's based in any dysfunctionality.
- During moments of emotional pain, we return to the age of unresolved trauma. If your partner is acting like a child, chances are that they're feeling like one.
- To truly heal, you need to address the cause, not just put a Band-Aid on the symptoms.
- If we don't address an issue, it'll keep coming up, as if it just happened yesterday, even if it too

place decades ago; the subconscious mind keeps no track of time, just unfinished business, to protect us.
- For a relationship to work, it needs work – from *both* sides!
- Crisis intervention can only help you through the crisis, not healing or growth.
- To change the outcome, you have to change the context, which led you to the wrong place.
- All wounds can be healed, but you have to be willing to go into the painful center to clean out the wound, or it will fester and keep causing pain.
- Always be clear on your goal; if healing your relationship is your goal, focus on that, and avoid attacking each other, via criticism, contempt, defensiveness, and stonewalling.
- If you don't apologize in a way that your partner understands, where you cover the key ingredients that they need to hear, your apology may feel worthless.
- An apology must never include the word "but" because it totally negates the wounded party's pain.
- Validating someone's pain and showing them that their pain impacts you, is the only way to move past your lips to their heart.
- Making an apology is just one half; accepting it is the other. Don't negate repair attempts.
- Challenge your thoughts before they become your beliefs – it's hard to fight those.
- Getting caught up in what-ifs makes you focus on things that may *never* happen, instead of working on what *is* happening.
- Always look for other possible explanations versus those that are closely connected to your

fearful filter. People think being suspicious will somehow protect them; when it does more harm than good.
- Trust is a fragile thing – it can't tolerate too many hits. Trust is also a two-way street: If someone is trying to be trustworthy, do what you can to be trusting.
- Forgiveness is a gift you give yourself.
- Forgiveness is giving up the need for sufficient punishment.
- Living with uncertainty versus erroneous certainty, is the only way of having a fair shot at saving your relationship.
- Holding on to a grudge is like eating poison and expecting the other party to die.
- Owning your feelings and managing them is healthier than guessing at someone else's feelings and managing *them*.
- Opening up to each other, both in and out of bed, keeps your connection strong.
- Mind-reading can be dangerous – try to share what's on your mind, instead of allowing your partner to assume the worst.
- If you pay more attention to your past versus your present or the future, it's like driving a car by looking in the rear-view mirror – you're bound to crash.
- Validation of feelings doesn't mean you agree on the subject matter. It's just an empowering way to connect – so why fight it?
- Assuming the victim status gives up control over a given situation.
- Every "victim" ends up becoming a persecutor at some point, when they start to attack the other party. Recognizing that and giving up both roles

is the only way of stepping out of the drama triangle – you never win if you stay in it, solo or as a couple.
- If you're stuck in a given situation, ask yourself what benefits you might be reaping, and what will it take to become unstuck – if you don't know, how can you expect your partner to know, and make things right.
- People who grow up in drama often seek it out – albeit subconsciously – because it makes them feel that everything is normal/familiar. If they don't see drama, they can become worried that something's wrong, or the passion is gone, so they may end up creating it; at times for no good reason.
- Being judgemental never accomplishes anything – it can only create a rift.
- The more someone invests in their recovery, the farther they get, the less likely they are to undo what they worked so hard to accomplish.
- No one is responsible for your happiness, only *you* can make yourself happy; but others can certainly make you unhappy – it's important to know the difference!
- If your partner gets easily triggered or becomes hypervigilant, it could be because their reality took them to places they never thought possible, which can make anyone paranoid. It's like the person who battled cancer but is now remission – any future lumps or hint of similar symptoms will terrify them more than the average person.
- Know each other's love and sex languages to love and pleasure in a way that's well-received.

- If you have each other's back, matter to each other, and are there for each other, all else will fall into place.
- Focus on what's important for the relationship, not either party, so you'll always stay on the same side, without any resentment!
- If you fill up each others emotional bank accounts, you'll be able to withstand a lot of stuff. If there's nothing to draw on, then you'll feel emotionally bankrupt. And trust me, emotionally bankrupt people live in a state of constant fear.
- Life is a beautiful journey, where you should look for detours, not stop at dead ends.
- If you journey together, you have a witness to your adventure; if you journey alone, you can get lost, and your stories will die with you.
- Recovery and healing from a betrayal is a lot of work; but nothing is more rewarding than that labour of love. You'll end up in a better place than where you began – but both parties have to show up for the ride!
- If you can focus on taking care of each other's feelings, even during your toughest talks, you'll stay on track.

The preceding tips are just a small sampling of the wealth of helpful information and advice contained in Rebecca's book **Overcoming Betrayal**. Although the thread throughout the book is on dealing with infidelity, there is an absolute treasure trove of general relationship advice – and I highly recommend you pick up copy and learn how to make your relationships the best they can possibly by to everyone's benefit.

Everything in Your Life is Interconnected:

A key factor behind many business failures often outwardly appears to have little to do with the business itself. But when personal relationships are in trouble, the impact on your business can be truly devastating.

Business executives, normally driven to succeed, now find their focus divided between work and an unhappy personal life. Their thoughts at the office often stray to a marriage or love life in trouble.

They become preoccupied dealing with rocky, unstable relationships, deep personal dissatisfaction, emotional pain, perhaps even depression. Much of the time once devoted to business matters is now spent on unhappy relationships - possibly even legal battles and lawyers.

It should come as no surprise that many failed marriages are closely followed by failed businesses - or vice versa. It's inescapable: Your business life and your personal life are components of your whole life - trouble on the home front all too often impacts the business front.

You need secure, loving relationships to succeed in all aspects of your life. This is especially true of married business leaders - but it also holds true for many single entrepreneurs who can easily fall prey to volatile relationships and become preoccupied with a time-consuming quest to find personal happiness that ultimately takes its toll on the degree of time and effort they can put into their business life.

Great Advice! / Michael B. Davie

Splitting your focus between business and personal life can often undermine both halves of your whole: Keeping your focus sharply on business while devoting little thought to your personal life may initially help business. But as your personal life suffers you can be sure it will inevitably invade your business.

You're likely already familiar with an array of business books that focus purely on building commercial success - but what you may really need is advice on building and strengthening loving personal relationships, so that your entire life is successful.

Renowned psychotherapist Victoria Lorient-Faibish is a relationship expert who has helped people from all walks of life - including many business folk - improve their personal life and relationships. She's helped many build their lives on a solid foundation of a successful personal life. Much of her advice is available in her breakthrough book **Connecting – Rewire Your Relationship-culture** (Manor House).

I caught up with Victoria as she took time out from her busy practice to hold back-to-back book-signing events at major Toronto bookstores. It was a great opportunity to meet the author, chat with her and get an autographed copy. For those who couldn't make it out to the event, other bookstores in Toronto and in major cities across Canada are stocking special autographed copies of her book (and it's available worldwide at Amazon and other online retailers).

Simply put, Victoria Lorient-Faibish would like to help create healthy relationships now! **Connecting: Rewire Your Relationship-culture** is about changing what isn't working to create a new, unique, personalized, choice-filled relationship-culture that you consciously bring into your adult relationships.

"Rewiring your relationship-culture involves understanding that your brain forms new neural pathways every time you develop a new way of doing something, especially if you practice the new behaviour often. It's nature's way of supporting us when we try to make positive changes."

"By rewiring your relationship-culture," she adds, "you'll be able to: move past multi-generational dysfunction; know and honour yourself fully; understand all the rules for dating in a healthy, empowering way; spot relationship dysfunction such as co-dependency, commitment phobia and narcissism; set good boundaries; utilize my pre-marital checklist; and learn the fundamentals for long-term, passionate relationships!"

Where It All Starts: Family-Culture

Victoria notes your family-culture is all you know in the beginning. It influences all aspects of your life. This is something you engage in without thinking. It is something that gives you a sense of community, belonging and family — when it is working for you. When it is not, it may cause you to feel unhappy.

It can also exert undue pressure on you to conform and fit into what your family knows and has done for generations. Family-culture includes the emotional baggage handed down through generations that profoundly affects the life of any given family.

The relationships, such as between parents and children, brothers and sisters, grandparents and grandchildren, are the real meat of the issue, and from where a family-culture derives. These relationships influence how a person turns out and how they interact in their own adult relationships. The family-culture has a profound effect on your relationship-culture.

Victoria observes: "What you experienced in your family dynamics growing up is largely what you will replay in your adult relationships. On the whole, we come from tribes, our families, with unique ways of doing things, and these patterns, habits and ways of communicating and relating are what you have metabolized as your family-culture, and it lives deep within your consciousness."

"The unresolved issues, hurts, traumas, family patterns, secrets, shames, triumphs, jealousies, abandonments and fears are all part of your particular family-culture that profoundly inform how you interact in your adult relationships and that infiltrate your relationship-culture."

Here again, I would urge you to read Victoria's book Connecting – Rewire Your Relationship-culture to fully benefit from this relationship expert's advice.

As a registered psychotherapist, keynote speaker, author, relationship expert and life and wellness coach with a master's degree in educational psychology and a Toronto practice, Victoria has spent the past 25 years inspiring people to find their self-culture, rewire relationships; step into their personal power / embrace their life purpose.

Victoria is also a registered member of the College of Psychotherapists of Ontario, certified member of the Canadian Counselling and Psychotherapy Association, a reiki master, and a board-certified polarity therapy practitioner and teacher.

Create a successful Family Life:

Communication in any relationship, including family relationships, is key to making it all work out, notes Blythe Ward, critically acclaimed author of ***Stepping Up to a Happy Stepfamily***. She notes:

"The stepfamily is not the only type of family that deals with change as their children develop emotionally and physically. "Cycles of life" happen in all families. All families must nurture their partnerships so they develop positively, and adjustments to their own individual life stages need to be made. The stepfamily deals with all of these natural life progressions while they grow. You may think you are going crazy, but you are not. You are dealing with the normal and continuous change of your stepfamily as well as the natural and continuous changes in life itself."

"There are, however, some fundamental actions you can take that will help make your partnership or marriages work well. Here are some ideas that are valuable for all married or partnered couples, regardless of whether there are stepchildren involved."

Blythe Ward has taken a special interest in stepfamilies and strategies to give them the best chance of success for over 20 years. Her experience as a stepmother, therapist and researcher has motivated her to share these strategies in a straightforward and easily read book. She is confident of the stepfamily as a loving nurturing entity and is committed to that message.

Great Advice! / Michael B. Davie

Blythe has a varied background having been born in Yellowknife, NWT moving to Edmonton, Alberta as a young person.

She attended the University of Alberta receiving a B.A in Psychology. Post graduation she worked as a social worker and then returned to University of British Columbia for an Education Diploma. Having moved back to Edmonton, she raised her two young boys while teaching children with special needs at Royal Alexander Hospital.

She also had business experience in running a modeling agency. In 1983, she moved to Ontario and continued her work as a special needs education teacher. She wanted to follow her passion to be a therapist and took night school completing her Masters of Education in Counseling Psychology at University of Toronto with which she established her own private counseling practice.

Blythe's personal experience with stepfamily parenting came when she married a man with three young children and together they created a stepfamily of seven.

It was clear that the stepfamily was a unique experience and Blythe researched extensively on writings in the field, she focused much of her counseling with step family issues. Blythe enjoys doing workshops and lectures on this subject.

All told, Blythe Ward brings more than 20 years of experience to her work as an expert in the art and science of building happy stepfamilies. Her book ***Stepping Up to a Happy Stepfamily*** is the culmination of a heartfelt focus on the topic that has endured for many years. As a stepmother, therapist and researcher, Blythe has a profound understanding of the challenges stepfamilies face and she is determined to share her message of hope with people struggling with demands of managing an "instant family."

Blythe believes a stepfamily can be a loving, nurturing entity. And the strategies she sets out in her book are focused on giving stepfamilies the best possible chance of success. I highly recommend her book. Here's an excerpt:
Blythe's Tips for Stepfamilies – and All families:

Keep your eyes on the big picture. Sit down together and make a plan for the future together and discuss how you see the next five years together. Talk about your individual goals first, and then discuss your goals for your new family. This way you will not be *assuming* that your partner is on the same page as you, and you are less likely to crash into a major disappointment at an emotionally vulnerable time.

Talk, talk, and talk! Set a specific time each day or week to stay connected to each other so you are connected and in tune with what is happening in each other's daily lives.

Compromise! And learn to say "sorry." Sorry can go a long way towards defusing anger and bridging misunderstanding.

Look for opportunities to support each other. We know that men and women might prioritize things differently but they both need conversation to help them feel understood and to understand their partner, a stable family environment, sexual fulfillment and affection, companionship, and respect for how he/she makes a living.

Remember that your partner isn't responsible for your happiness. You need to find ways to support yourself, too. Keep your expectations of your partner's role in your life in line, because he or she can't make up for everything that goes wrong in a day.

Remember who you are as a person. Keep your own friends, hobbies and beliefs. Find things that give meaning to your life. Make yourself happy by nurturing yourself.

See "couple" friends. Friends can help and support you as well as share social experiences. They can be an inspiration for new ideas and ways to deal with life issues.

Work to understand each other's feelings. You don't have to fix them or change them… But each of us needs to be heard.

Don't become submerged in "busyness." Remember to compliment each other, encourage each other, and give each other little gifts to show you appreciate each other. Help each other with the household jobs that need to get done, and hug or touch each other every day.

Try not to discuss difficult topics when you are angry. Everyone is sensitive to conflict and we each have triggers for our fears. But remember that good marriages have some conflict in them because both partners need to speak up and feel that their needs are being met. It is how you speak up that matters.

Accept the fact that it is ok to agree to disagree sometimes. Not all issues are solvable. If you agree to disagree, then try to let it go. Repeat, "It is what it is."

Treat your partner better than you would a best friend. Remember that children grow up and move on, as they should. You deserve to have a future together after the home nest is empty, too.

Most of all… have fun together. Laughing is good for the marriage and the whole family.

Finding time for many of the above suggestions is a skill in itself. Make it a priority. Get babysitters or arrange for short private times together each week. Date night is not over rated and it gives both of you something to look forward to each week."

Helpful hints for the couple in a stepfamily:

- **Never stop acknowledging how hard it is to be a stepparent.** Support each other verbally and emotionally.

- **Make sure you have each resolved how you feel about your ex- partners.** Strong negative or positive feelings about the ex-partner will interfere with the bond between the new partners. Seek counselling if this is an issue for one of you.

- **Schedule time together.** There is so much going on in a stepfamily that if you don't make time together a priority, it won't happen. It doesn't matter what you do together, just do it. This time will help to form the "glue" that holds you together as a couple over the years.

- **Try to coordinate "visitation" times of children, if possible, so that you can have weekends together without anyone's children.** It is very good for the couple to have time together and also to allow you both to recharge for the following week.

- **A parent always misses their own children a lot when one parent has their children with them**

- **and the other one does not.** Take this into consideration when you are making plans.
- **Lack of enough time is a huge issue for stepfamilies.** You need to be concerned about your kids, my kids, the family, me and us. Figure out a plan together to manage your family time. Remember that the most difficult times are organizing the mornings, pre-dinner time, and the weekends.
- **Often couples in stepfamilies are still dealing with legal issues.** Spend less time and energy discussing and dwelling on these difficult legal issues. Allot 15 minutes a day to discuss them, and then get on with your daily lives. Your relationship is not structured on the issues from the past.

There's no "magic potion" to guarantee your new life together will be easy and free of strife. But if you're each dedicated to each other and the children for whom you are responsible, there is a good chance you can have a relatively harmonious, and often very fun, life together. It takes a bit of work and a whole lot of creativity. And it is possible.

Here are some thoughts on money issues that may help:

- **Discuss your views on money before you get married, or as soon as possible thereafter.** Partners often have different thoughts on money issues. Make sure you understand how each of you will manage all of your expenses. Surprises about money are not helpful and can create mistrust between partners.
- **If finances were a problem in your first marriage, be sure to discuss those issues so that you don't accidentally make the same mistakes**

again. Sort out together any debts you're bringing into the marriage and how to repay them.
- **Most of the time, often due to divorce, there are previous financial obligations for one or both of the partners.** Resentment can grow unless both partners understand and accept this responsibility.
- **Marital agreements are more common these days.** You would be well served by going through the process of negotiating and putting a marriage agreement in place. Adult children often need their parent's financial support too. They seem to be more supportive of the new family if they know their inheritance is not greatly affected.
- **Ideally, each partner should have their own personal bank account as well as a joint family one.** Incorporating the practice of making sure each partner has some personal money is important. Where incomes are unequal, such as where one parent stays home to look after the children, it is helpful to put money into that partner's personal account each month. This will give them a feeling of independence, and equality, as well as help them to feel valued.
- **Always discuss big purchases with each other before you make them.**
- **If the financial system you are using is not working, figure out why and try a new way to deal with this issue.** There are many choices.
- **Set up a budget and try to stick to it.** Arguing about money can wear a relationship down.
- **Parents are role models.** Parents teach children how to manage their own money. Try to be careful what you teach them by example.

Communication:
Here are three easy steps:

Step one: Express your thoughts with the famous assertiveness statement that starts with "I." Such as "I" feel, or "I" think, or "I" hope or "I" wonder, etc. For example…

"I feel badly because I can't seem to get a handle on the house work."

Step two: State what you need from that person.

For example:
"I need all of you to put your dishes into the dishwasher after each meal.

Step three: Ask if you have their help or cooperation.
For example:
"We would like to know that you can help us with this. Will you?"

We all need to "speak up" so that we can be heard and understood. What is important is *how* we "speak up." In any family, everyone's thoughts and feelings are important, no matter their age. Here are some important thoughts to consider when communicating in your stepfamily:

Sometimes talking about their feelings on the issue will help.

For example:
"I know you mean to do it and then you get busy, but I would appreciate you trying harder to remember. Can you do that?"
Another example:
"I don't think you are telling me the whole story. I need you to explain why you slammed the door on your sister just now."
Use "we" or "us" whenever you can to reinforce that all of us are in this together.

For Example: "I would like us to find ways to change this situation."
Take a deep breath before you state what you want to say. That way you have a few seconds to think your communication through before speaking.

When you listen carefully, stop what you are doing and look at that person. Your job is to understand what they are thinking and feeling.

Sometimes it is just helpful to tell them "I hear you." You don't have to agree, but you can still listen to what they have to say. They will feel they have been heard.

Many people find it helpful to mirror what they have been told. That way, if they have misunderstood the situation, they can be corrected right away.

Start with "I hear you say that…"or "So you want me to know that…" This works because if you've misunderstood the message, you can be corrected right away.

Empathizing with what you have been told can initially open up a communication, especially with a child. You don't have to fix it, but you can understand, e.g., "I can see that you are really sad about your brother breaking your toy train. That is hard."

Plan a time and place in the house to talk for a short time with your partner each day. If some days this is impossible, arrange to talk on the phone.

Try not to go days without communicating. There is just too much change happening in a stepfamily each day.

Sources of Great Advice:

Samantha Cervino: smbalternativehealing.me
Author, *The Dragonfly Effect*

For many years **Samantha Cervino** worked with children diagnosed with ADD, ADHD, Asperger, Dyslexia and Autism. She has changed and improved the lives of many children, as well as countless clients in her practice of energy healing and self-development coaching. She is committed to helping guide her clients and humanity toward achieving a well-balanced life.

In addition to being an accomplished leader in her field of understanding and shifting human emotions through Reiki, EFT Tapping and continuous studies in self development, the human mind, achieving personal success and the universal laws, Samantha, is able to help others learn what it takes to meet their goal and show them how to tap into their endless potential.

She is a blogger, published author, and Wellness Universe Ambassador, who motivates through her work on social media by sharing great insights by the world's greatest minds and teaching her audience about the importance of gratitude and affirmations. Samantha believes in giving back to humanity. For many years she has sponsored a child in Africa. She also gives of her time to serve in her community as a peer counsellor at the Women's Centre. As well, she facilitates support groups for changing results. As a master energy healer, Samantha is committed to the personal success of her clients and is often quoted for her stated belief: "Life is to be felt, not planned."

For more information visit Samantha Cervino on LinkedIn and access her blogs, or email her at samcp10@gmail.com

Sources of Great Advice:

Rebecca Rosenblat: www.relationshipandsexuality.com
Author, *Overcoming Betrayal*

Rebecca Rosenblat is well known as one of Canada's leading relationship, sexuality, and healing experts, who has reached a captive audience of millions across North America. Some of Rebecca's accomplishments include, hosting three TV shows, two call-in radio shows, running sold-out seminars, keynoting at various conferences and trade shows, authoring several books and advice columns, and becoming a popular voice with the media.

As a psychology graduate from the University of Toronto, Rebecca's credentials earned her an incredible opportunity to work at Canada's most prestigious psychiatric facility - The Clarke Institute. During this time, she became a popular international lecturer, published in several medical and psychiatric journals, and nurtured her counselling skills. After years of service at the Clarke, Rebecca shifted her healing focus from psychiatric illnesses to relationship issues, becoming involved in sex therapy, relationship counselling and life coaching.

Rebecca was chosen to create, produce and host two highly rated, call-in, radio shows - a nightly, sex talk show for Mojo Radio (AM 640), and a healthy lifestyle show for CHWO Radio (AM 740). On the TV circuit, Rebecca is currently hosting a live, call-in show, Sex @ 11 with Rebecca.

Contact Information for Rebecca Rosenblat:
http://www.relationshipandsexuality.com
Email: rebecca@relationshipandsexuality.com

Sources of Great Advice:

Victoria Lorient-Faibish: www.visualizationworks.com
Author: *Connecting – Rewire Your Relationship-culture*

Victoria Lorient-Faibish would like to help create healthy relationships now! Connecting: Rewire Your Relationship-Culture is about changing what isn't working to create a new, unique, personalized, choice-filled relationship-culture you consciously bring into your adult relationships.

"Rewiring your relationship-culture involves understanding that your brain forms new neural pathways every time you develop a new way of doing something, especially if you practice the new behaviour often. It's nature's way of supporting us when we try to make positive changes. By rewiring your relationship-culture, you'll be able to: move past multi-generational dysfunction; know and honour yourself fully; understand all the rules for dating in a healthy, empowering way; spot relationship dysfunction such as co-dependency, commitment phobia and narcissism; set good boundaries"

Victoria has spent the past 25 years inspiring people to find their self-culture, rewire relationships; step into their personal power / embrace their life purpose. She's a registered member of the College of Psychotherapists of Ontario, certified member of the Canadian Counselling and Psychotherapy Association, a reiki master, and a board-certified polarity therapy practitioner and teacher.

Contact Information for Victoria Lorient-Faibish:
Phone: 416-916-6066 or 844-332-3254
Email: info@visualizationworks.com

Sources of Great Advice:

Blythe Ward / Author Speaker Therapist:
www.blythward.com
Building Happy Stepfamilies

Blythe Ward brings more than 20 years experience to her work as an expert in the art and science of building happy stepfamilies. ***Stepping Up To A Happy Stepfamily***, is the culmination of a heartfelt focus on the topic that has endured for many years. As a stepmother, therapist and researcher, Blythe has a profound understanding of the challenges stepfamilies face and she is determined to share her message of hope with people struggling with the demands of managing an "instant family."

"If you want to feel more confident as a stepparent and learn how to develop practical skills to address daily challenges, this book is for you! Blythe has "cut to the chase" in delivering a book that will truly raise your awareness about how successful stepfamilies work… breathes refreshing, loving, and positive insight into the world of stepfamilies."
– Patrice McKenzie M.S., Ed. C.N.H.P. Therapist, Mother, Step Mother

Contact Information for Blythe Ward:
www.blythward.com
Email: blythe40@me.com

About the Author

Michael B. Davie is the critically acclaimed author of literally dozens of books (including some that were ghost-written for others).

He's also President-CEO of both Manor House Publishing Inc. and Rockport Records International Corp., critically acclaimed author of more than 20 books, and an award-winning career journalist and editor, whose professional career spans more than 40 years with major publications, including The Toronto Star, The Globe & Mail and The Hamilton Spectator plus several national news organizations and freelance work with numerous magazines and periodicals.

Great Advice! / Michael B. Davie

About the Publisher

Founded in 1998, Manor House Publishing Inc.is renowned for it's array of outstanding authors, including novelist and singer-songwriter Ian Thomas (mega hits include Right Before Your Eyes, Coming Home, Painted Ladies, Hold On and more – plus hit songs written and performed by Chicago. Manfred Mann, America, Bette Midler, Santana); plus Spoonfed – My Life with The Spoons by frontman Gord Deppe telling the story of his rise to fame with The Spoons, their hits Nova Heart; Romantic Traffic; Tell No Lies; and, Those Old Emotions and their years touring with The Police, Simple Minds, Culture Club and many others.

Manor House business titles include *Grab Success by the Horns* by Barry Siskind (best-selling author of Bumble Bees Can't Fly); *The Street Smart Marketer*, *Leaders* – and more, while Self-Help titles include bestsellers on the Law of Attraction – and current releases *Connect With the Divine You* by Tanya Penny; *The Dragonfly Effect* by Samantha Cervino; *Overcoming Betrayal* by Rebecca Rosenblat, *Connecting* by Victoria Lorient Fairbish; and, *Stepping Up To A Happy Stepfamily* by Blythe Ward. Recent novels include *Coven of Soul Sisters* by Laverne Stewart and *Little Sister* by Vince Fernandez.

Manor House Publishing Inc.
www.manor-house-publishing.com
905-648-2193

www.ingramcontent.com/pod-product-compliance
Lightning Source LLC
Chambersburg PA
CBHW071853070526
44583CB00016B/1668